HyperCard®
Stack Design Guidelines

Addison-Wesley Publishing Company, Inc.

Reading, Massachusetts   Menlo Park, California   New York
Don Mills, Ontario   Wokingham, England   Amsterdam   Bonn
Sydney   Singapore   Tokyo   Madrid   San Juan

© Apple Computer, Inc., 1989
20525 Mariani Avenue
Cupertino, CA 95014
(408) 996-1010

Apple, the Apple logo, HyperCard, and Macintosh are registered trademarks of Apple Computer, Inc.

APDA, HyperTalk, IconMaker, and ResEdit are trademarks of Apple Computer, Inc.

Macworld is a registered service mark of Apple Computer, Inc.

ITC Zapf Dingbats is a registered trademark of International Typeface Corporation.

Linotronic is a registered trademark of Linotype Co.

MacPaint is a registered trademark of Claris Corporation.

Microsoft is a registered trademark of Microsoft Corporation.

Porsche is a registered trademark, and Porsche Speedster is a trademark, of Dr. Ing. H.C.F. Porsche, A.G.

POSTSCRIPT is a registered trademark of Adobe Systems Incorporated.

Varityper is a registered trademark, and VT600 is a trademark, of AM International, Inc.

Simultaneously published in the United States and Canada.

ISBN 0-201-51784-1

BCDEFGHIJ-DO-89

Second printing, October 1989

Contents

7 Music and Sound 133

Figures and Tables

CHAPTER 3   **Introducing People to Your Stack 51**

CHAPTER 4   **Graphics in Stacks 63**

About Stack Design

HUNDREDS OF THOUSANDS OF MACINTOSH® COMPUTER OWNERS ARE ALSO HyperCard® users. The power and flexibility of HyperCard allow virtually anyone to become an "application author," creating custom stacks for personal use, for business or education, or for commercial distribution as retail or "shareware" products.

But all stacks are not created equal. If you've looked at many stacks, you've probably encountered some that don't seem to work right, some in which you soon get lost, and some that have cluttered, confusing card and background layouts. In such cases, the stack design—or lack of it—has diminished the stack's effectiveness.

The key to designing an effective stack is to focus first on who will be using it and on what the stack will do. When the stack seems simple and straightforward to the users, even if it's doing complex tasks, they perceive the stack design as effective.

Graphic design and user interface design

Two aspects of design are especially important in building HyperCard stacks: graphic design—the appearance of cards and backgrounds—and user interface design—how users interact with the stack and navigate within it from one place to another.

As you consider these two aspects of design, you will probably want to address questions like these:

- "What is my stack trying to accomplish?"

- "Is the purpose clear to my users?"

- "What's the best way to lay out this stack? This card?"

- "What kind of button should I use here?"

- "If I use this kind of arrow, will users know what I mean?"

- "How do I tell users what's going on?"

Answers to these questions will depend on your stack's users, the subject matter of your stack, and the stack's style of presentation. A solution that's appropriate for one stack may be completely inappropriate for another. This book will give you general guidance for making design decisions. User testing can then help you pinpoint any remaining specific problem areas in your stack.

What you should already know

To get the most out of this book, you should have read and understood the *HyperCard User's Guide* and should already know how to create cards, buttons, fields, and stacks. The features described here are based on HyperCard version 1.2 and are largely similar to earlier versions.

What's in this book

This book discusses how to create useful, effective stacks with emphasis on design and navigation. It does not cover how to write scripts in HyperTalk™.

- Chapter 1 presents a brief summary of the stack design guidelines.

- Chapter 2 discusses how to make stacks that are easy to navigate.

- Chapter 3 discusses how to introduce people to your stack.

- Chapters 4 through 7 cover the specific elements of HyperCard and how to use them:

  - graphics

  - buttons

  - text and fields

  - music and sound

- If you've never built a stack before, read Chapter 8; it gives a step-by-step example and discusses collaborative stack building.

- Chapter 9 presents a synopsis of Apple's *Human Interface Guidelines* in the context of stack building.

- Appendix A discusses special market considerations: creating stacks for international use and for use by disabled people.

- Appendix B contains the Stack Design Checklist — a tool for your own stack building.

- Appendix C lists books you might want to read for further information.

User groups

Ask your dealer for the name of a Macintosh user group near you. If you live in the United States, you can call (800) 538-9696 for the name, address, and telephone number of up to three Macintosh user groups in your geographic area.

Regardless of where you live, you may also contact one of the following organizations:

- The Boston Computer Society
  One Center Plaza
  Boston, MA 02108
  USA
  (617) 367-8080

- Berkeley Macintosh User's Group
  1442-A Walnut Street #62
  Berkeley, CA 94709
  USA
  (415) 849-9114

Either of these organizations can provide you with the name of a Macintosh user group near you. You can also join either of these groups or ask them for information on starting your own Macintosh user group.

The Guidelines

THIS CHAPTER PRESENTS NINE PRINCIPLES TO GUIDE YOU AS YOU DESIGN AND build HyperCard® stacks. Designing a stack is like designing any other software application. The first three guidelines concern what you should know about any stack before you begin creating it. The next three guidelines present the major considerations you should keep in mind while planning and building a stack. The final three guidelines remind you to pause and study each stack and to keep experimenting with new approaches until the stack comes out the way you want it.

A Stack Design Checklist that incorporates these guidelines is included in Appendix B.

The guidelines in brief

The list below summarizes the guidelines; the following sections explain them more fully.

1. Decide who your users are.

2. Decide what the stack's subject matter is and what it is not.

3. Decide how to present the subject matter to your users.

4. Make your stack easy to navigate.

5. Introduce people to your stack.

6. Integrate text, graphic design, and audio design.

7. Plan on changing your stack several times.

8. Test early, test often, and listen to your reviewers.

9. When you're finished, check the stack one last time.

Guideline 1: Decide who your users are

Who are your users? The answer to this question affects your design decisions more than any other factor. You may have one user (yourself), or you may have thousands. Your user group may be all alike, or may vary widely. Some users may be familiar with HyperCard, while others may never have touched a computer.

Defining your users will help you focus your design. As you develop and build your prototype, you'll want representative users to test the stack for you and suggest improvements. If you're building a stack for architects, for instance, you can assume certain conventions, such as blueprint notation, will be understood by the audience, and you'll want architects to review the stack at various stages to confirm your assumptions.

Imagine how you would vary the design of a stack for the following audiences:

- third-graders
- third-grade teachers
- department managers in an advertising agency
- commercial stack designers
- all employees of a car manufacturing plant
- computer-science graduate students
- Israeli, Arab, Bolivian, and Chinese geologists
- hearing-impaired artists
- filmmakers and animators who've never used a computer
- your family and friends

Visualize your users. Describe one or more of them. Think about their assumptions, needs, hopes, and fears. What do they already know—and what don't they know? Why would they be using your stack, and in what context?

What previous experience do they have with computers, with the Macintosh® computer, and with HyperCard? How well do they know the subject matter? Will they be using the stack alone or with other software? Will they be learning it alone, or as part of a training class? Are your users in different countries? Are they disabled in some way?

Imagine designing a stack about dinosaurs for third-graders. This audience consists of both boys and girls who on the average have a low reading level and short attention span, who need frequent positive reinforcement, and who need a simple interface. Now consider designing the same stack for paleontologists, who know the subject matter, have a high reading level and long attention span, and want an interface that lets them access the information in many different ways. Although your subject matter is the same, the two audiences would require different solutions to meet their needs.

You may need to do some research to find out who your stack's users will be. Talk to your colleagues. Do some research. Use the Stack Design Checklist in Appendix B to help you define users for your stacks in detail.

Guideline 2: Decide what the stack's subject matter is and what it is not

Now that you know your audience, define and focus your subject matter. The more focused you are, the easier your design decisions will be. Deciding your subject matter has three components:

- Decide the purpose of your stack.

- Decide how much information you will cover—all the inventory in the store, or just the sporting goods merchandise, for example.

- Decide what resources the stack will require and estimate how long it will take to build. If you don't have much development time, you may have to limit the amount of subject matter.

Designing "a budgeting stack for first-level managers," for instance, is difficult, because the problem is so vague. It's much easier to design "a budgeting stack for first-level managers that tracks monthly expenses—but not capital costs—by actual amounts, against outlook and plan. The stack also must accept general ledger input from the company's mainframe computer." The latter is more specific, and therefore easier to design.

Now consider how the design for this project would change if you had to fit it onto one 800K disk. Perhaps you'd need to eliminate some capabilities, to save disk space. Consider again how the design might change if you had three months to develop it, or only three weeks. Perhaps three months would allow you to write a custom **XCMD** (an **external command,** written in another programming language and called by HyperCard) to exchange data with the mainframe computer, but three weeks would not be enough time.

As you define your subject matter, its nature will begin to influence how you present it. A budgeting stack, for example, may suggest presentation methods such as spreadsheets, financial planning charts, or graphs.

Guideline 3: Decide how to present the subject matter to your users

In deciding how to present the subject matter to your users, you may choose one presentation method and then discover as you go along that another one works better. Some ways to present a stack's subject matter are as a slide show, animated movie, desktop presentation aid, tutorial, game, or software application.

Play around with ideas. Sketch ideas on paper and on the screen. Ask other people for opinions. Choose a presentation method and draw a "map" or diagram of the stack: does it look clear or confusing? A method that's perfect for one stack may be inappropriate for another. A presentation requiring users to take one specific path through the stack might be perfect for a training stack, for example, but inappropriate and frustrating for an informational reference stack.

To choose a presentation method, study the stack's subject matter and intended audience. For example, a product demo for in-store retail customers might bring to mind a "rolling slide show" presentation that repeats itself automatically. Showing the same product's features to upper management, by contrast, might suggest a "table of contents" presentation, allowing the presenter to jump immediately to the features managers wanted to see.

Consider using a metaphor. A **metaphor** is an identification between a real-world object and parts of your stack that share the object's characteristics. The standard Macintosh interface, for example, uses a desktop metaphor with documents, file folders, and trash cans. Because people already know how the objects such as trash cans work, they easily learn and remember how to throw files away.

Familiar metaphors help users quickly grasp complex ideas. Imagine you were building a stack to control a stack full of pictures of ships. These are some stack metaphors you might choose.

- A picture-book metaphor, in which users look up categories of ships in a table of contents, click to go to a specific chapter, and then use buttons to turn pages in the book.

- A videotape-player metaphor, in which users click buttons on a control panel to rewind or fast-forward the tape to see different ships.

- A shipyard metaphor, where users arrive at the docks and specify which tour they want to take. They're given a chart on which to select different sails, rigging, engines, and hulls. Their tour, then, shows them only the ships that have those specified components.

Use metaphors only when they make your stack easier to use. Sometimes there is no real-world object that's similar, so the most appropriate design is one that uses no metaphor at all.

Choosing a presentation method is a pivotal design decision. Changing the basic form or presentation of your stack can solve many problems at once. Early in the process, it's easy to change the form and presentation of the stack; as development continues this becomes harder to do. Therefore, focus primarily on the presentation method in your initial testing and reviews.

When you are designing the presentation method, you are working on the stack's user interface. **User interface** encompasses all the elements that determine how a stack looks and how a user interacts with it (such as presentation, graphic design, and navigation); it does not include that stack's basic functionality. In the "stack full of ships" example above, for instance, the stack's basic function is to provide ship pictures. But the user interfaces in the three solutions—book, videotape, or tour—let the user experience that functionality in very different ways.

Guideline 4: Make your stack easy to navigate

Navigation, the part of the stack's user interface by which users move around within the stack, is the most important component of stack design. If users are confused or frustrated when trying to move around in a stack, they will quit, no matter how useful the subject matter.

With other media, such as books or videotapes, people have physical clues about how much of the information they've seen: books have page numbers and become heavier on one side as pages are turned, for instance, and videotapes have counters and gather tape on one reel as the tape is played. But with stacks, users need other ways of knowing how much of the information has been covered.

To navigate effectively, users must know their options, the stack's size and general layout, and the stack's rules. Well-designed navigation makes getting around within a stack seem simple and intuitive. In general, the less users have to think about where they are or what to do next, the more they can concentrate on the subject matter.

Users move through stacks as if they are moving through rooms. Think of how you learn your way around an unfamiliar house, or office building, or museum, or cave. Users can get lost in stacks that seem like mazes of tunnels. Stacks with clear signposts, maps, names of rooms (cards), and simple layouts are easier to comprehend, remember, and navigate.

Navigation methods vary, depending on the stack's users, subject matter, and method of presentation. Whatever its design, a stack's navigation system must address five user needs:

- Context: What's in this stack?

- Location: Where am I now within the stack?

- Destination choices: Where can I go?

- Travel methods: How do I get there?

- Progress indicators: Where have I already been?

Often one device will satisfy two or more of these needs simultaneously. A stack map, for instance, can satisfy all five user needs by showing the stack's layout, using highlighting to indicate where the user has already been, graphically indicating "You are here," and providing buttons by which users can travel to their next destination.

Using a real-world metaphor is another way to give users integrated navigation information. A tape-recorder metaphor, for instance, conveys a linear context, with travel options of "Rewind," "Fast Forward," "Play," "Record," "Jump to Frame," and "Erase."

Visual effects are a subtle, powerful way to reinforce your navigation choices. If you use them consistently—always using a dissolve to move to and from the main menu (or table of contents), for instance—users get additional information about their location and direction of movement.

Some components of navigation are menus, maps, frames, textual reminders, you-are-here indicators, travel buttons, and progress indicators. Chapter 2, "Making Stacks Easy to Navigate," discusses these elements in detail.

Guideline 5: Introduce people to your stack

When people first open a stack, they need to learn its purpose, how it works, and how to use it. They need to learn the rules of the environment you've built. People who have used the stack before, on the other hand, will want to get directly to the heart of the stack and to get help only when they ask for it. By making the opening short and the explanatory information either brief or optional, you can introduce beginners without slowing down experts. These are some methods for introducing users to a stack:

■ Make your stack simple to use, so minimal learning is required.

■ Include a title card that describes the stack's purpose. If you're using a menu or table of contents, present it next, and have the first item be "Help" or "How to use this stack." If you're not using one of these methods, insert a one-card description of how the stack works between the title screen and the main stack.

■ Get the user doing something quickly in the stack, such as clicking a button or typing a name.

- Provide an explicit introduction to the stack. Give introductory information in small chunks, so users don't have to assimilate too much at once.

- Don't keep secrets from users; tell them how your stack works.

- Provide specific help for your stack—not just links to the HyperCard Help system—with a button that's always available. Put buttons in the help system, so users can find what they need without reading through long screens of information. Use graphics, animation, and sound to illustrate the help concepts. Explain your stack's buttons and remind users how to move around the stack.

When designing your help system, follow the same principles that you use to design an effective stack. The sort of help you provide will depend on your stack's audience and purpose and on the results of your user testing.

Most people learn best by doing. One strategy to get the user actively involved is to provide introductory information in small chunks, so that in order to continue, the user must do something. Another strategy is to put nonthreatening options early in the stack. Buttons such as "Introduction," "Help," "About this stack," "Click here to begin," and "Click here to continue" are especially inviting.

Don't feel obliged to be fancy. As with other areas of design, the best solutions are usually those that seem simple and obvious to the user. If your stack opens with a title screen, introduction, and menu, for instance, people will not even notice the design. If the same stack opened without warning to the first functional card, however, people would not know what to do and would perceive the stack as being hard to learn how to use.

Chapter 3, "Introducing People to Your Stack," provides a detailed discussion of different methods for getting users started with your stack.

Guideline 6: Integrate text, graphic design, and audio design

Most people work with four major elements in their stacks: they create buttons and place them on backgrounds or cards, they experiment with the graphic design, they write the text, and they compose or capture the sounds for the stack. But unless these elements work together harmoniously, users have trouble figuring out what the stack is supposed to do and how they are supposed to use it.

When text and visual elements work together, less text is necessary. Instead of saying, "Icons that are diamond-shaped, with a small shadow, indicate hints," for instance, the stack designer could reduce the text by saying "Icons like this indicate hints" and then showing a picture of the icon.

When text, graphic, and audio elements give a consistent message, the user gets an integrated, stable impression of the stack and its subject matter. Here are some points to keep in mind:

- Design consistent card and background layouts.

  Create a consistent background structure for related cards, put navigation buttons on every card, and keep the buttons in the same place throughout the stack. Put elements common to every card in the same place and group buttons by function.

  Imagine an invisible grid over your screen. Block some sections out for text, others for graphic images. Use the largest or most focal part of the screen for the most important information; put navigation buttons on the edges of the screen. See Chapter 4, "Graphics in Stacks," for more information.

- Write for the screen, not for paper.

  A stack is not a book. Written material for the screen usually needs to be concise and tightly structured to fit into meaningful chunks. It's tiring for people to read from the screen, so use readable fonts and succinct text. Design the layout and appearance of your text just as you would any other graphic element. Study magazine advertisements for ideas about graphic layout and placement of text. Chapter 6, "Text and Fields," discusses writing for the screen more fully.

- Provide high-quality graphic and audio design.

  If your graphics or sounds are amateurish, people will assume your stack's function is also hastily or badly designed. Today's audiences are accustomed to media that provide sophisticated sound and images because of their exposure to television, motion pictures, and multimedia performances and presentations. Chapter 4, "Graphics in Stacks," and Chapter 7, "Music and Sound," discuss the use of these elements in more detail.

- Incorporate the general design principles of Apple's *Human Interface Guidelines.*

  Two of the most important principles of interface design are *forgiveness* and *user control.* Expect users to make mistakes, and forgive those mistakes; give users a second chance and help them correct their errors. Also, give users control over what to do with your stack. Provide users with options and information, but let them have control of which sections to explore, which buttons to click, and when to quit. The details of this and other principles are discussed in Chapter 9, "Human Interface Design."

Guideline 7: Plan on changing your stack several times

Building a stack, like developing any other software, is a cyclic, repetitive process. You're likely to change your stack a lot in the beginning. You might try out different structures and metaphors, different introductions and openings, different navigation methods, and different presentation styles.

One approach that can often save time and trouble is to think of several solutions, design all of them to a certain point, and then choose one for further development. This method can be faster and less frustrating in some cases than designing a single solution, implementing it, and then having to revise the design, reimplement it, and so on.

Your goal is to produce the best possible final stack, not to defend your first beloved idea. Points at which your stack is likely to change are

- in the design stage, as you're first figuring out your users, subject matter, and basic presentation method

- later in the design stage, after you have a working prototype of the stack

- in development, as you repeat the "build–test–revise" cycle.

Many stack developers find that when they enter the production phase, with the stack's interface set and its features frozen, they have a workable but awkwardly built stack, so they stop and rebuild it cleanly from scratch. Whatever your approach, expect change.

Guideline 8: Test early, test often, and listen to your reviewers

You may be tempted to wait until your stack is "perfect" before you show it to anyone. To do so, however, could mean disappointment and a lot of additional work. It's better to get feedback early and often by establishing regular tests or reviews of your stack-in-progress. Testing or seeking reviews can mean several different things—showing the stack to one person or to a group of colleagues, sending it out for informal review, or setting up a structured, formal test. It's important that you test; you can go about it any way that works for you.

Don't explain the things you're trying to test. If you want to find out whether users can navigate through your stack easily, don't give them verbal instructions beforehand for navigation. Use participants who are similar to the people who will be using your stack.

By watching and listening to your testers and reviewers carefully, you can uncover mistakes when they're still relatively easy to correct. You'll also probably discover that your testers will offer good ideas that you can add to the stack as you refine it.

Listen to what people tell you. If they say the stack is confusing, don't argue; say, "Thank you. What in particular is confusing?" The point is to find out how others perceive the stack, and not to defend your ideas.

Watch what people do when they try to use your stack. See what pitfalls people find, and what solutions they try, without offering your comments. If several users try the same solution, consider providing that capability in your stack. If several users misunderstand an aspect of your stack, redesign it.

Test your help function as well as the stack. Ask testers whether the help system provided the information they needed, and what information they wanted but couldn't find. If your testing shows that your users need to get help often, perhaps your stack has other design flaws. Maybe the structure is too confusing or is not well suited to the subject matter.

To make your user testing most effective, repeat it throughout the design and development of your stack. Some good points at which to seek reviews are

- after you know your user, subject matter, and presentation style (your design may exist on paper only, at this point)

- after you have a working prototype (including links) of the stack that gets across its purpose

- after you have your first, and each subsequent, fully working version of either the entire stack or its main sections

- after you've made any big change, especially in the stack's underlying presentation method, introductory elements, or navigation system

- when you think you're ready to deliver the stack to the users

For more information about testing, see the Stack Design Checklist in Appendix B.

Guideline 9: When you're finished, check the stack one last time

This step is the exhaustive, meticulous final exercise that can make a stack gleam. No matter how much you've checked before, check the production version again. Enlist new eyes to help. Deliberately do the wrong thing and see what happens. Bring in new testers and offer a reward for every problem they find.

Details make the difference. Your stack should have

- no typographical or grammatical errors

- text and graphics that relate to each other (no mismatches)

- buttons that all work

- scripts that all run without crashing and that produce the intended result

- logical presentation sequence to cards (so that the `Show all cards` command produces orderly results)

- alert and dialog boxes that all work (check all options, including Cancel)

- navigation and links that all work and are connected to the correct destinations

- consistency throughout the stack

- no glitches with sound or animation timing on any Macintosh model

Check to make sure that everything's linked, that users can't get stuck in a dead end, and that scripts don't bomb. Check that copyright and legal notices have been inserted. Verify that no viruses exist on the master disk.

When you have a final disk with no bugs, put everything associated with this project—all your disk versions of the stack, scripts, XCMDs, printouts, hand-drawn designs, design plans, Stack Design Checklists, and notes—into order while they're fresh in your memory, and save them.

When you build your next stack, you may want to copy this design plan, use some of the graphics, or copy one of the scripts that didn't make it into the final version of this stack. This organization is invaluable if you need to have someone else revise or rewrite your stack, or if you need to revise it a year from now.

The disk is ready to duplicate and distribute. Celebrate!

Summary

Developing stacks is a cyclic process of designing, getting reviews, and revising. By following the first three guidelines as you begin—deciding who your users are, what your stack's subject matter is and is not, and how to present the subject matter to your users—you give yourself a basis for making all other design decisions and prevent wasted development time.

Most of your design and development time will be spent in the details of making your stack easy to navigate, providing an introduction to your stack, and integrating text, graphic design, and audio design. Don't wait until your stack is "perfect." Test it early, test it often, and listen to your reviewers so you don't go astray. To incorporate reviewers' comments and your own observations, plan on changing your stack several times.

When you're finished, check the stack one last time. Other software developers have learned that it's better to ship software late than to ship it with major bugs. This final check makes sure your stack communicates your subject matter to your users in a way that's clear and effective.

Making Stacks Easy to Navigate

A N EFFECTIVE NAVIGATION SYSTEM ANSWERS FIVE BASIC QUESTIONS ABOUT the stack for users.

- What's in this stack?

- Where am I now?

- Where can I go?

- How do I get there?

- Where have I already been?

The navigation system you choose will depend on your stack's users, subject matter, and style of presentation. In general, the fewer levels and less movement the stack requires, the simpler navigation will be.

Stack structures

The nature, purpose, and presentation of information in a stack help determine its structure. The need for easy, efficient navigation can also help determine the stack's structure, particularly if the stack contains complex information or a variety of tasks.

The term "stack structure" really means *perceived* stack structure—the way users think of the stack. The order in which users see the cards is determined by how you link the cards, which may be different from the physical order of cards in the stack. If a stack's perceived structure is simple, users will find a stack easy to navigate even though it has several levels and a number of different cards and backgrounds.

Five common ways to structure your stack are discussed in the sections that follow. They include

- linear structures
- tree structures
- network structures
- single-frame structures
- combination structures

Linear structures

A **linear** stack structure is one that encourages—and possibly forces—a user to move through it in a straight line. Linear stacks provide a single logical path through the information they contain. Examples of linear structure include a nonbranching tutorial stack, in which the user must learn several things in a specific order, and a slide-show-with-music stack, in which the images appear in a predetermined sequence.

A linear structure would also suit a "zooming stack," in which a user zooms from outside the galaxy, for instance, into the solar system, earth, Europe, Scandinavia, Norway, Oslo, down onto the statues near the Oslo harbor.

Navigation in a linear stack consists primarily of movement forward and backward. Most linear structures also benefit from a return-to-start option. Figure 2-1 shows the basic structure of a linear stack. The squares represent cards, the arrows represent travel possible within the structure.

■ **Figure 2-1**   A linear stack structure

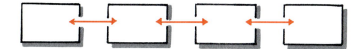

A variation of the linear structure is the **jump-linear** structure that offers the ability to jump out of the linear sequence to a given "home-base," choose a new point within the stack, and jump to it. A stack showing common marine mammals, for instance, might use a jump-linear structure. Imagine the animals arranged in standard taxonomic order, one per card, with one additional card listing all animals in the stack. A user could jump to the main animal list from any other card, then select which mammal to study next. (Jump-linear stacks are technically a form of tree structure, but users perceive them as similar to linear ones, hence their name.) Figure 2-2 illustrates a jump-linear structure.

■ **Figure 2-2**   A jump-linear stack structure

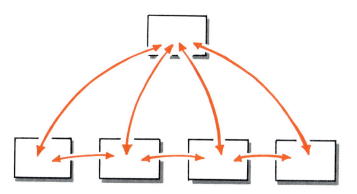

Linear structures are useful when you want users to have only one path through the information. If you want them to have primarily one path but with the additional ability to jump to any given point, use a jump-linear structure.

Linear structures are not useful when you want users to be able to select different paths and branches within the stack, depending on various decisions, actions, or preferences. In these cases, one of the nonlinear structures will provide better navigation.

Tree structures

A **tree** stack structure is one that lets users choose among several branches to follow the path that interests them. An organization chart is essentially tree-structured, as is a reference book with many levels of subsections (such as chapters, first-level headings, second-level headings, and so forth). In a stack, this might be represented with a menu metaphor that in turn utilizes submenus. A tutorial stack may be tree-structured if the user is given explicit choices, such as "Would you like to review the material before taking the quiz?" or if the designer has built in implicit choices, such as "If the user has failed the quiz, then go to the Remediation branch; otherwise, go to the Next Topic branch." Figure 2-3 shows an example of a tree stack structure.

■ **Figure 2-3**　A tree stack structure

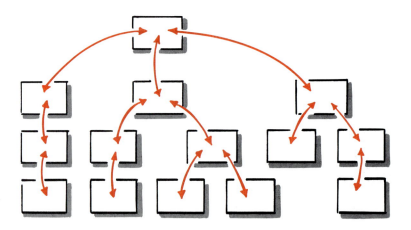

Navigation in tree-structured stacks lets users move forward and backward within a branch, return to the most recent forking point, return to start, and possibly jump to the stack map. This navigation is shown in Figures 2-3 and 2-4.

■ **Figure 2-4**   A tree structure users can navigate easily

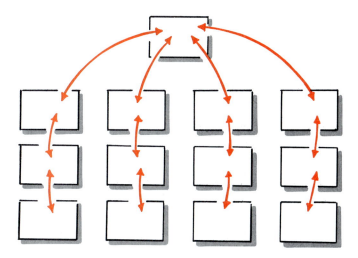

People find it confusing to cross from one branch to another without going back "up" first, since few real-world objects work that way. It's not possible, for instance, to enter one apartment building, go upstairs, walk through a door, and find yourself in the apartment building across the street.

Users can keep track of stacks like the one shown in Figure 2-4. but they get lost quickly in structures like the one in Figure 2-5. Novice stack builders or novice hypermedia designers frequently make this design mistake.

■ **Figure 2-5** A tree structure users find confusing

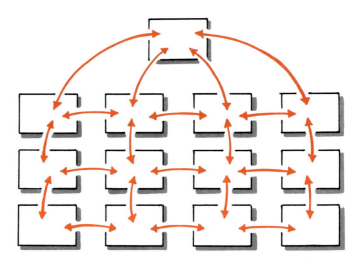

Tree structures are useful for stacks in which the information naturally divides into a few ordered hierarchies. They have power because people are used to seeing information arranged in this way.

Tree structures are less useful for stacks in which the information has so many levels that the users can easily get lost in the hierarchy, or in which the information has connections not only within a branch, but between nodes of different branches.

If the users of your stack need to make many choices before determining a path, a single-frame structure may be preferable (discussed later in this chapter), or possibly a combination single-frame/tree-structure.

Network structures

A **network** stack structure is one in which the information is linked without a strict hierarchic order; users can explore in many different ways. Buttons in these stacks may lead to other cards or other stacks. For example, an adventure game might be done as a network stack. So might a stack depicting airline routes of a major carrier. Figure 2-6 shows a stack with network structure.

■ **Figure 2-6**   A network stack structure

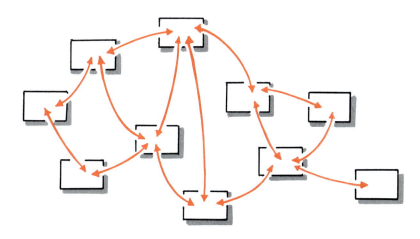

Navigation in network stacks depends upon the subject matter. There may be heavily used cards that serve as reference points (or hubs), as in the most heavily trafficked cities on an airline route. Or, you may decide to present a stack map or menu as a way for the user to organize the information.

Network stacks usually provide the ability to move forward to a new card, move backward to the card most recently visited, to return to a given card (or cards), and to jump to the stack map or menu.

Network structures are useful for collections of information that must be arranged to allow users the maximum "travel" options, such as the airline-routing example.

Network structures are not useful when information would fit a simpler structure, because networks are often hard for users to understand and navigate. As with tree-structured stacks, if you find the network structure evolving simply because of the number of choices your user must make, consider using a single-frame structure instead.

Single-frame structures

Single-frame structures are those that appear to the user as a single card on which all actions take place. In fact, the stack consists of several cards, but the user has no sense of traveling. Navigation in single-frame stacks is particularly elegant because it appears to be nonexistent.

Display stacks. The purpose of these stacks is to display a large graphic or text field whose content changes according to the user's choices. The display area remains constant. A stack showing American Sign Language fingerspelling, like that shown in Figure 2-7 for instance, might let the user choose letters in one area of a card, then display the corresponding signs in a fixed other area.

■ **Figure 2-7**   A single-frame display stack

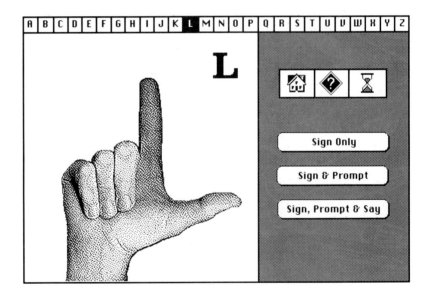

Filter stacks. In these stacks the user chooses one or more "filters" by which to sort the remaining information. For instance, in a stack for identifying flowers, such as that shown in Figure 2-8, the user might "sift" through all possible flowers by asking to see only those flowers of a certain color, with certain petal and leaf shapes, found in a certain part of the country.

A filter stack sometimes functions as the **front end,** or part that the user sees first, to a combination stack. The user might specify flower characteristics, for instance, then go to a linear stack of all flowers meeting the specified criteria.

Filter stacks are increasingly useful as the amount of data in the stack grows, since the search capability they provide is increasingly critical. A stack containing information on 10 flowers, for instance, would not need the filter capability as much as a stack containing information on 5000 flowers.

■ **Figure 2-8**   A single-frame filter stack

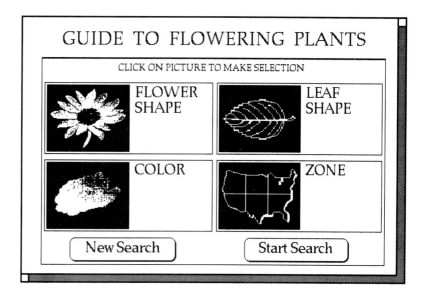

See-and-point stacks. In these stacks the information is first presented on one card; when the user clicks on the area of interest, that area appears to temporarily enlarge (as with an overlaid pop-up field or an iris-open visual effect). When the user has finished with that area, one click shrinks the enlargement back to its initial size.

This technique is frequently used in educational stacks, where users can choose to learn about as many or as few parts of a diesel engine, say, as they wish. Again, this can be used in combination with other stack structures, but it provides a simple navigational metaphor. Figure 2-9 shows a see-and-point stack in which the user clicks on photos of old friends to see current information about them.

■ **Figure 2-9**   A single-frame see-and-point stack

If your information fits into a single-frame structure, take advantage of it. Users have no sense of "going" anywhere, so they can't get lost; navigation is not a problem. Single-frame stacks are useful when the user must first make a variable number of choices, before determining content or path. Single-frame structures make elegant front ends to other kinds of stacks, because they seem simple and intuitive.

Single-frame stacks are not useful when there are too many kinds of information, or too much to present to the users without them getting confused. In these cases, you may decide to add a "wrapper": add an introduction and teach the user about the stack, before showing the single-card stack itself.

Combination structures

A **combination** stack structure is one that combines two or more types of structures. It may have a single-frame front end for choosing filters or paths, then use a tree structure for traversing those paths. Or, it may be technically a network structure, but within the network are long linear chunks.

The kind of information and presentation will help determine the structure. Your guiding principle should be simplicity and usefulness: is this the simplest stack structure that is useful to the user? The user needs to be able to comprehend the structure, and also to move around it at will. You might start with one structure, then modify it to make it more usable or comprehensible.

Combination structures are useful when the information doesn't naturally lend itself to simpler structures such as a linear or tree structure. Often, an innovative interface that feels simple to the user is actually a complicated combination stack to the stack builder.

Combination structures are not useful if they confuse the user or if your information fits a simpler model.

Aids to navigation

Navigation may consist of very few elements, such as two arrow buttons in a linear stack, or it may consist of several elements that together help the user move around within the stack. Screen location of the elements plays an important role in letting the user know how to navigate. Some common navigational elements are menus, metaphors, textual reminders, stack and card names, "you-are-here" indicators, travel buttons, and progress indicators.

Menus

Menus, also known as topic lists or tables of contents, can provide both context and ways for users to measure their progress. The term *menu* is being used here loosely to refer to any list of stack sections. It's typically a main screen containing text and possibly visual labels for the different sections of the stack.

The users see the menu early and return to it frequently to orient themselves and to navigate through the rest of the stack. The menu should roughly mirror the stack structure and should list all main parts of the stack. If each main stack section itself contains a number of topics, consider using submenus at the beginning of each section.

Figures 2-10, 2-11, and 2-12 show three different types of menus. The first one relies solely on text to tell the user about sections of the stack. The second, in Figure 2-11 uses both text and graphics but focuses on text. And the third, in Figure 2-13, uses both text and graphics, but emphasizes the graphics. For different stacks, different mixtures of text and graphics are appropriate. In designing a menu, it's most important that users can quickly and easily see their options.

■ **Figure 2-10**   A text-only menu

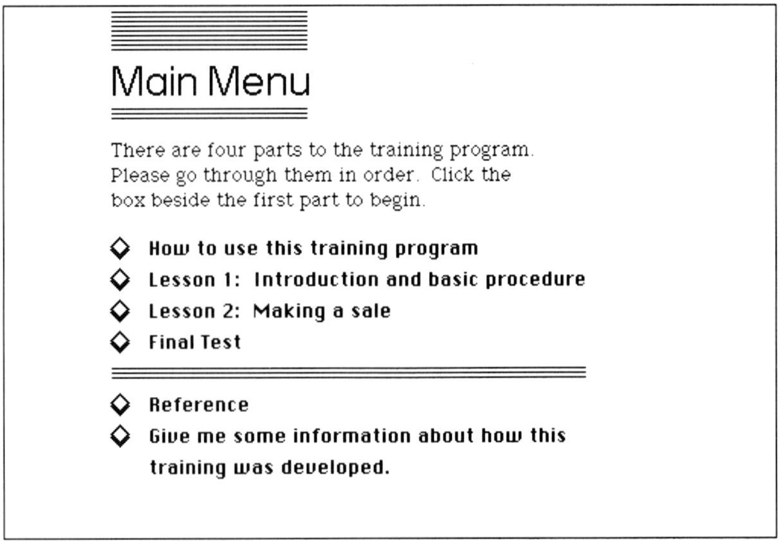

Main Menu

There are four parts to the training program. Please go through them in order. Click the box beside the first part to begin.

◇ **How to use this training program**
◇ **Lesson 1: Introduction and basic procedure**
◇ **Lesson 2: Making a sale**
◇ **Final Test**

◇ **Reference**
◇ **Give me some information about how this training was developed.**

A special consideration when designing text-only menus is to make sure the user knows which words on the screen are buttons. Your written instructions should always tell the user what to click. You can provide graphic clues as well by making clear button shapes, like the standard rounded rectangle HyperCard button shapes, around each menu word; by using a distinctive typeface for button names; or by providing a small box, circle, or other symbol next to the menu word. In any case, there should be some designation that invites interaction and that distinguishes menu words from ordinary text.

■ **Figure 2-11** A text-and-graphics menu emphasizing text

■ **Figure 2-12**   A text-and-graphics menu emphasizing graphics

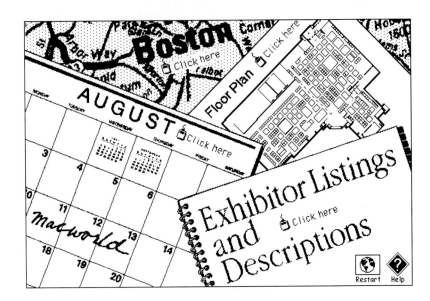

Menus are useful when your stack has some natural topic groups, such as different subject headings, branches, kinds of information, or kinds of presentation. They're also appropriate when your information is not layered too deeply and has simple linear or tree-structure connections.

Menus may not be useful when your stack has hierarchies several levels deep (users may forget which menu they're on), or when the information is structured in a network or combination stack, where users need more information about how things are connected.

Stack maps

Stack maps are powerful navigation components because they satisfy many user needs at once. A **stack map** differs from a menu in that the map provides a visual representation of both the stack pieces and the connections between those pieces. The best stack maps are also "live": users don't just look at the map, but can click areas on it to travel to any chosen point.

Stack maps are especially useful when your stack has tricky or complex connections or a complicated structure.

Stack maps aren't particularly useful in stacks with linear or conditional navigation paths, such as step-by-step tutorials.

Figures 2-13 and 2-14 show two stack map possibilities. The stack map in Figure 2-13 shows the contents, structure, and linkages of the stack. It's easy to locate any topic in relation to the rest of the stack. The stack map in Figure 2-14 provides similar information, but gives graphic reminders of the cards as well. A user who wants to return to the card with the picture of the bicycle on it, for instance, can find the desired destination without having to remember the name of the card or section.

■ **Figure 2-13**   A stack map

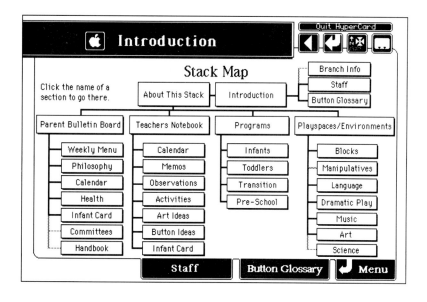

■ **Figure 2-14**   A stack map with graphic navigation reminders

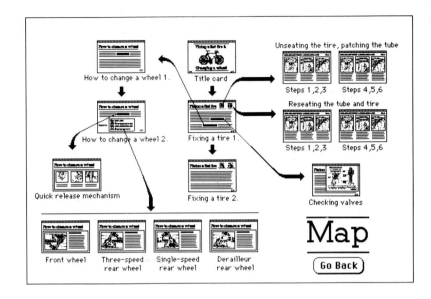

Metaphors

Real-world metaphors can help convey the user's navigation options. A floor plan, for instance, contains and conveys more information than does a list of rooms. Graphic images of books, cassette-players, film projectors, control panels, or maps furnish additional information about how the subject matter is laid out and how it can be traversed.

Figure 2-15 shows a movie-review stack in which navigation is presented simply as a set of possible actions, with no underlying metaphor. Figure 2-16 illustrates that same stack, using a cassette-player metaphor to help the user remember the navigation choices and general model.

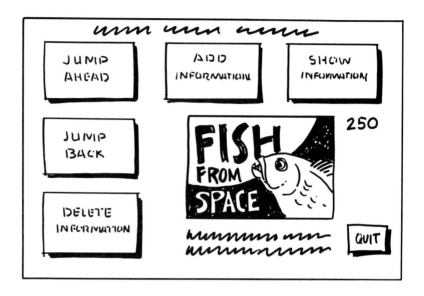

■ **Figure 2-16** The same navigation choices using familiar tape-player metaphor

Your subject matter will often influence your choice of metaphor. Housing information lends itself to metaphors of floor plans and real estate listings. Travel information lends itself to maps, schedules, and brochures. Stacks that ask the user to choose among several variables may lend themselves to control panels.

Stack structure can also influence metaphor choice. Linear stack structures can be modeled by cassette players or film projectors. Tree structures can be modeled by organization charts, stack maps, or books (with different chapters and subheadings).

Textual reminders

There's nothing wrong with simply telling the user the necessary navigation information. For a given stack's audience, purpose, and presentation, textual reminders may be the best choice. A tree-structured stack might call attention to the buttons and arrows, saying, "To revisit any part of this section, choose a button below. To go to another section, choose a button to your right." Textual reminders lessen the amount of information users have to remember in order to use the stack, so that they can concentrate on the stack's content. Figure 2-17 shows an example of explicit textual reminders. The user has two choices, and the text explains what they are and how to proceed.

Ready for a quiz?

At this point, you can either go on to
Quiz 1 or go through the "Basic
Procedure" section again. Click the box
beside your choice.

◇ 1. Quiz 1
◇ 2. Repeat Basic Procedure Section

**Stack names and
card names**

Names that identify stacks, menus, sections, and cards are an effective way
of letting users know where they are at any given point.

Always name your stacks. Even a single-frame stack should have either the
stack name written at the top of the card or an opening card that gives the
stack's name.

Name your cards, as appropriate. If, throughout your stack, you provide a
button called "Return to Menu," be sure to have the name "Menu" appear on
the menu card. Naming cards is also a good way to differentiate between
two cards that look similar. Figure 2-18 shows an example menu screen as it
was first designed, and then with its name added, as shown in the final
version.

■ **Figure 2-18** An unidentifiable screen, the same screen with a clear title, and the final version

Don't give one item two different names. For instance, if you call the main screen simply "Overview," don't have a button that returns to it called "Return to Hardware Overview" or, worse, "Return to Main Menu."

As a scripting technique, it's safest to refer to objects by ID, however, because the ID number is unique and never changes. A card's number will change if you cut and paste the card, for instance, and a card's name can be duplicated by copying the card. An additional advantage of using an object's ID in your scripting is that HyperCard will run faster. The resulting increase in speed is especially striking in large stacks.

"You are here" indicators

A good way to reinforce navigation is to provide both context and location information simultaneously. Provide a map, for instance, that also indicates "You are here." Figures 2-19 through 2-22 show different ways of using location and context indicators. In Figure 2-19, the stack shows different rooms of the house. To prevent the user from getting disoriented, a constant floor-plan icon in the lower right indicates which room is currently on screen. In Figure 2-20, part of the graphic itself, the monkey trail and sign, is highlighted to provide location and context. Figure 2-21 provides the missing information in a familiar book metaphor, by supplying both the current page number and the total number of pages. And Figure 2-22 presents the name of the current location in the text, "Reconnaissance Aircraft."

Figure 2-19   The floorplan tells the user "You are here"

■ **Figure 2-20** The highlighted sign tells the user "You are here"

■ **Figure 2-21** The page number tells the user "You are here"

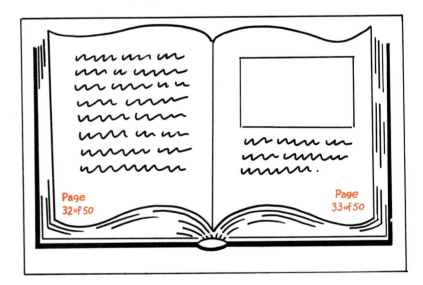

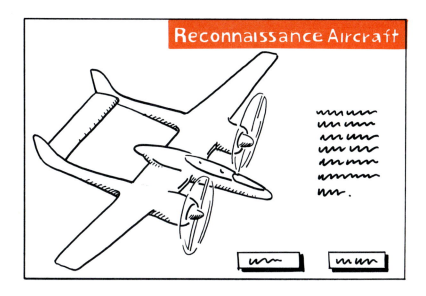

Titles and names are an unobtrusive and intuitive way to give users information about their location. If you keep the card titles in a set location on the screen and make them visually consistent, the user will develop the habit of referring to that screen location for orientation. In Figure 2-22, for instance, other vehicles in the same stack would be named in the same white-on-black lettering in the upper right.

If your users are getting lost or confused in the stack, adding card titles is a simple and sure improvement to let the user know "You are here." If your stack has subsections within sections, you may want to consider providing two kinds of titles, one to let users know the general section they're in, and another to tell them which subsection.

Buttons that let the user travel

Whenever your users need to travel in your stack, provide buttons. Even if your audience consists of expert HyperCard users, give them buttons; it's courteous and effective. The card on the left in Figure 2-23 would require users to remember or look up a means of keyboard navigation, which would be confusing and frustrating. Stacks without traveling buttons are like cities without cars or buses, forcing the user to walk the whole time.

■ **Figure 2-23**   A card with no visible travel options and the same card with obvious buttons

Buttons designed *solely* to let the user travel (such as "go forward" or "go back") should appear different from buttons that that let the user do other things (such as "show printers" or " calculate test score"). By making travel buttons consistently different in appearance and location from operational buttons, you'll save the user from having to figure out that there are different categories of buttons.

Use placement to differentiate buttons. Put navigation-only buttons in one area, and stack-usage buttons in another. Separate permanent navigation buttons from card- or section-specific buttons.

Use graphic design to further differentiate buttons. Make the buttons with which the user travels look different from, probably simpler than, the buttons for doing other things. Or perhaps use icons for the navigation-only buttons and words for the other buttons.

Figure 2-24 illustrates this concept. In the image on the left, all buttons are intermingled at the bottom of the screen, with little to differentiate the four navigational buttons from the three that are card-specific operational buttons. The middle drawing and the final version show a clear separation, with the permanent navigation buttons now moved to the upper-right corner of the screen.

■ **Figure 2-24**   Buttons all grouped together, buttons segregated by function, and the final version

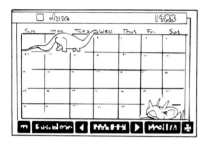 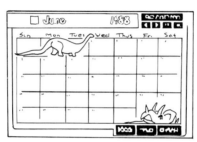 

For details on choosing and implementing buttons, see Chapter 6.

Progress indicators

Users need to know how much of a stack they've covered. Either you can tell them explicitly or you can give them tools to determine their progress themselves. If their travel within a stack is constrained, tell them explicitly how much is left. If they can determine their own travel, then give them a tool such as a map or gauge for judging their progress.

The navigation elements you've chosen to show context, location, or destination choices can convey progress as well. For instance, a book metaphor, "open" to page 33 of 100, tells the users they've progressed a third of the way through the stack. Other elements, such as a menu, stack map, or table of contents, can also serve this purpose.

You can provide custom visual progress indicators, such as gauges, dials, bars, meters, or checked boxes. If you reserve part of the screen to show a progress indicator or dial, users can judge their own progress. Figure 2-25 shows some possibilities.

■ **Figure 2-25**   Visual indicators of user progress

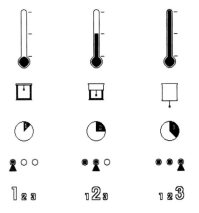

You can also tell users explicitly, with text, how much they've covered. A linear stack might contain statements such as this: "You have now finished section 1 and have two sections left."

Summary

In most stacks, users need to travel around, and they must do so without getting lost or confused. To navigate successfully, they must know the stack's layout, the means of travel, available destinations, and their own current location. You can provide this information with a combination of devices and graphic elements, all of which work together to give users the necessary information.

Sometimes the general metaphor or environment of the stack provides a framework for navigation. A television metaphor, for instance, can convey the notion of branching (changing channels) and then traveling through a linear sequence (watching a show), without having to provide a lengthy explanation.

As the amount of data in the stack grows, the navigation methods must become more sophisticated. Databases or applications on 656-megabyte CD-ROM disks require sophisticated searching, sorting, and traveling methods to prevent users from getting lost or overwhelmed.

Introducing People to Your Stack

THE HYPERCARD ELEMENTS YOU USE TO INTRODUCE PEOPLE TO YOUR STACK will vary, depending on your users, the stack's subject matter, and the method of presentation. In most cases, though, the users' needs are the same—they need to learn the stack's structure, purpose, and rules. They need to learn how to use the stack, how to navigate through it, and how to get further help.

Stack openings

A user begins to learn about your stack from the moment the first card appears on the screen. Don't waste those opening moments; they are your chance to start teaching the user naturally and to set the tone of your stack. If your stack opens with an ambiguous, untitled screen, the user's first impression will be "This is a confusing stack."

A well-designed opening accommodates needs of first-time users, but provides buttons or other options for experienced users to bypass the introductory information and go straight to their desired destination.

There are two common ways in which stacks open. One way is essentially a **static opening,** with a title screen, including copyright notice, possibly followed by some legal or credit information, and then by the main menu (the first item of which may be "Introduction").

Figure 3-1 illustrates a static opening screen for a stack on bicycle repair. When users open this stack, they are given its title and purpose, some copyright information, an "About" icon (the cartoon speech balloon in the lower-left corner) with which to learn more about the stack, and a pointing-finger icon to click for traveling forward in the stack.

A variation of the static opening uses a short animated beginning section before the title screen and main menu appear. (Keep in mind that long animated sequences can become annoying with repetition; if you have a long animation, give users the ability to bypass it.)

The other common way to open stacks is what's called **attract mode:** The stack opens to a rolling, inviting, animated, possibly audible display that attracts the user. On the screen are the words "Click anywhere to continue" or "Click here to see the stack."

The MacWorld® opening illustrated in Figure 3-2 uses an attract mode. When the stack is idle, it remains on the screen with the large words "Welcome to MacWorld" and the small words "Click on the world." The globe spins endlessly, providing movement and interest.

The stack doesn't open, however, or play the beginning animation sequence laid out in Figure 3-2, until a user initiates it After someone has clicked the globe, the animated sequence zooms down from planetary orbit to North America, to Boston, and eventually onto a table in the MacWorld exhibit hall.

An "attract-mode" opening is useful for demonstration or information stacks intended for use at places such as conventions, department stores, and building lobbies.

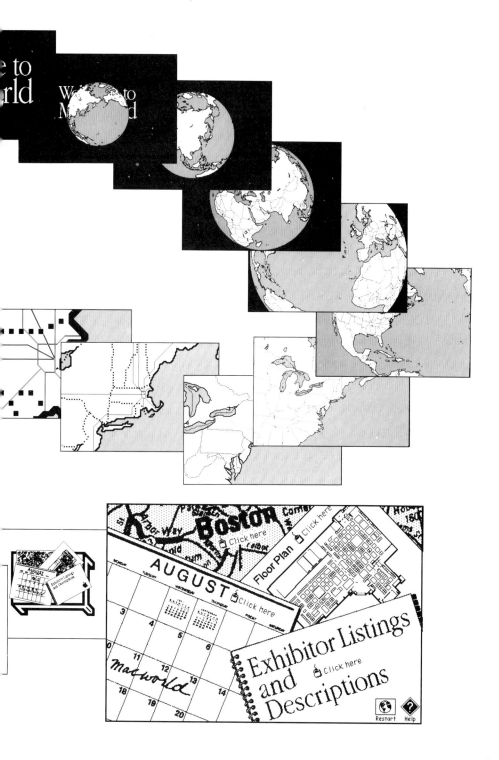

Early interaction

Most people learn best by doing, so it's good to get users involved quickly. People are likely to stay involved if they have some early successes, so get them doing something easy. Or, even better, have them do something easy that has spectacular results, such as launching a whizzy graphics-and-sound display when they press a "Show demo" button.

Invite users to begin interacting by providing click-to-continue buttons or by having them choose menu items. A natural dovetailing of the users' need to do something and your need to teach them about the stack can be accomplished by providing an interactive introduction to the stack.

When users do something successful right away, they feel confident and at ease, which is a positive beginning to their experience of your stack. Some people are timid about interacting with computers; by giving them an early success, you encourage them to try more challenging actions later.

Introductions

An introduction explains the stack's purpose as well as how to use it and how to navigate through it. The introduction should also tell users how to ask for more information if they forget the rules or get confused. Every stack needs to encourage interaction, whether it's designed for third-graders or adults and whether it's presented as a game, a control panel, a tutorial, or a spreadsheet.

You can make your introduction interactive. For example, if you tell users, "Clicking an icon like this will take you to the stack map," you have been informative but have not encouraged interaction. It would be better to tell users, "Clicking an icon like this will take you to the stack map. Try it now." Make the icon in the introduction a live button that takes users to a *copy* of the stack map, and on that copy write in big letters, "This is what the stack map looks like. For now, click anywhere to go back to the Introduction."

If some users of your stack won't be familiar with the Macintosh, your introduction may also need to teach basic techniques such as pointing, clicking, and, if pertinent to your stack, dragging. You'll probably need to introduce the idea of buttons and traveling. Describe your stack's navigation conventions, such as forward-arrow, backward-arrow, and return-arrow buttons (and what they mean in your stack) and any permanent buttons such as Help, Return to Start, Main Menu, Stack Map, Quit, or Home.

Beginning users won't know that some parts of the screen are "live" and others are not; to the innocent eye, all graphics are equal on a flat plane. You'll need to show that some areas are buttons, and that clicking them produces action or travel.

In short, your introduction should give the uncertain novice user the information and physical practice necessary to feel confident using and exploring the rest of the stack. It should provide a concise overview of the stack's content, teach the stack's structure, if necessary, and tell the user how to navigate. And, in accomplishing this, it should also give the user several easy, successful experiences interacting with your stack.

"About" boxes

An "About" icon button

"About" boxes are the screens of text that appear when the user clicks the stylized cartoon speech balloon icons. Although most people include the stack's title, purpose, and credits in the opening, some designers prefer to give the purpose and author information in an About box. Any subsequent click should close the About box.

Two factors you should consider when deciding whether to use this component are that information in an About box is less accessible to users than information presented openly, and that novice users may not recognize the meaning of the About box symbol. You could instead use a standard button named "About This Stack," if space permitted.

It's good to use an About box in a simple single-frame stack (in which all stack action appears to take place within a single frame), or in stacks in which visual space is at a premium. In contrast, an About box may break the visual "story" if you have a richly designed stack in which most information is presented openly.

The About box shown in Figure 3-3 illustrates a screen of text that would appear if a user clicked the About cartoon speech balloon icon. Note that, although the About icon is always a balloon, the text that it brings up can be simply text in a standard rectangular frame.

■ **Figure 3-3**   An "About" box, showing creator information

The About balloon, like the forward and backward arrows and the Home icon, is an icon with specific and expected uses. Use the About balloon only to show creator information about a stack. If you want a cartoon balloon coming out of a character's mouth, for instance, create your own instead of using the About balloon icon.

Stack-specific help

When users want help they almost always want it to be stack-specific or even specific to a particular task they are attempting (known as **context-sensitive** help). If your stack's help button sends users to the HyperCard Help, they may not know where they are or how to get back, and they are likely to feel betrayed by the stack's navigational system.

One way to differentiate your stack's help function from HyperCard Help is to choose a name other than "Help." For a stack called ExampleStack, for instance, you might name your help function, "How to use this stack" or "ExampleStack Help" or "Help for ExampleStack."

Generally, users will ask for help in one of the following circumstances:

- when they don't know or have forgotten what to do to perform an action

- when what they tried to do didn't work as they expected it to

- when they are lost

- when they don't know or have forgotten how to navigate

The help option should serve a tutorial and preventive function; it should not be the only repository of knowledge. Most user options should be available on the screen, not hidden off in the stack's help cards.

Some guidelines to remember about providing help to users are as follows:

- Help is never a substitute for good interface design. Don't explain a difficult interface—fix its problems. When you have made the interface clear, then develop a help system.

- Users shouldn't need help on how to get help. A help button should be visible and self-explanatory, and the information itself should be structurally simple.

- Make your help system interactive. Provide a quick, clear way for users to return to the point at which they asked for help.

- Organize the help information into chunks, so users can scan and select the information they want.

Reference points

Another way to orient users to your stack quickly is to provide a reference point—a sort of home base (but not the Home card). If you don't provide one, many users will treat one of the initial screens as a reference point, which could be confusing to them.

A reference point is a known place from which the user can get to other destinations. In a linear slide-show stack, the reference point may be the opening screen; in a tree-structure stack, the main menu; and in a network-structured stack, the stack map.

Although you may have hierarchies of reference points, such as menus and submenus, it can sometimes be confusing to have two competing reference points, such as both a menu and a stack map. If your design really benefits by having two reference points, however, choose one to be primary. Refer only to that single reference point throughout your stack's directions. Provide a button that's always named Main Menu, for instance, and have it always take users to the Main Menu card, not sometimes to the stack map. In your instructions, consistently say, "Return to the Main Menu when you're finished," not sometimes "Return to the stack map."

Focusing on a single primary point, such as a menu, gives users a single model of how to use the stack, without depriving them of the ability to use other tools, such as the stack map.

Summary

Users form impressions of stacks immediately upon opening them. To be most effective, your stack should introduce the user naturally to the stack from the moment it opens. You need to introduce the user to this stack as courteously and confidently as you would introduce a guest to your house or a new employee to your workplace. Tell users the rules of the stack, the shortcuts that they'll find handy, and the places to go for more information.

Provide good functionality, a good interface, and a good introduction, and people will find your stack easy and intuitive to use. User testing is a useful way to find out what topics or navigation mechanisms need to be introduced: watch what assumptions people make about how your stack works, then address those assumptions in the design and in the introduction.

Graphics in Stacks

I N STACK DESIGN, GRAPHICS ARE CRUCIAL AND PERVASIVE. NO LONGER
are graphics used only for decoration. In HyperCard stacks, graphics define
the environment and convey meaning.

In a printed book, if you changed the typeface, illustrations, and layout,
users could still tell they were reading a book. In a stack, however, changing
the graphic design, style, and images can mean the difference to the user
between reading a book, watching a movie, playing a game, taking a test, or
using simulated software.

Graphic design is the art of presenting text and images to communicate
clearly. A good graphic solution can make navigation simple and obvious.
Graphic design in a stack consists of several components: visual style, card
layout, metaphor, screen illustrations, scanned images, icons, typography,
visual effects, and animation.

Visual style

Every stack has an overall visual style. This style is reflected in the button design, the text-font choice, the illustrations, and the "look" of all the elements together. The look may be slick, sophisticated, childlike, historical, futuristic, playful, businesslike, or a thousand other possibilities.

What's important is that your stack's visual style is consistent and that it is suitable for

- your audience
- your subject matter
- your style of presentation

It's impossible to decide on a visual style if you haven't determined these three elements.

The visual style should fit the subject matter and audience. If your audience is business people, your visual style may be clean and sophisticated. If your subject matter is American history, your visual style may be rough-hewn, emulating woodcuts and quill-writing. If your presentation choice is a game, your visual style may be cartoonish and playful.

Either your navigation or your presentation may employ metaphors. If so, the kind of metaphor will influence the visual style.

Figure 4-1 shows information presented in four different visual styles. In the upper left, the salmon information is presented in a plain HyperCard style, for a general audience. In the upper right, the visual style is adjusted to suit an audience of children, with the penmanship title lines and large cartoon hand.

The lower left version is a visual style designed for a scientific audience. Note that this visual style allows for more and denser information than the child-like one, for instance.

The lower right card shows a visual style designed for a more avant-garde audience. The information is broken into chunks and presented piecemeal for the user to browse.

■ **Figure 4-1** Different visual styles. From left, top row first: plain HyperCard, childlike, scientific, "avant-garde"

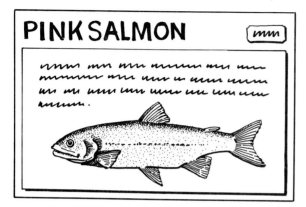

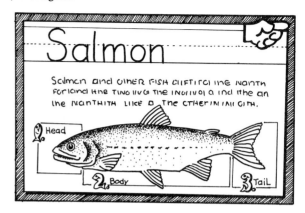

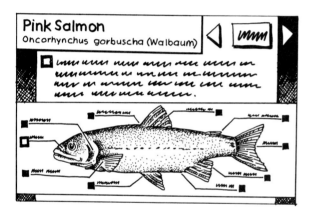

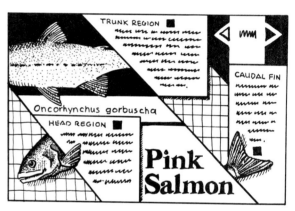

Stacks with different visual styles look and feel very different to the user. The next four illustrations show the different effect that different visual styles can convey.

The stack shown in Figure 4-2 uses a visual style that, if there is such a thing, "looks like HyperCard." It uses one of the standard backgrounds available with every copy of HyperCard—the spiral-bound, tabbed notebook. It also uses the standard HyperCard arrow, return-arrow, and Home button icons. Even the illustration of the tree shown here can easily be created using the standard HyperCard Paint tools.

■ **Figure 4-2** A stack that "looks like HyperCard"

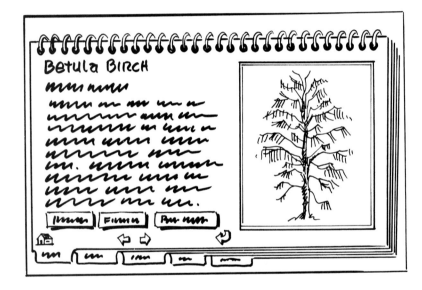

The stack shown in Figure 4-3 simulates the standard Macintosh interface for training purposes. Notice how different this visual style is from that of the preceding example. It's important that in any such simulation, the environment is clearly identified as a simulation (as this screen does by having a text box floating on top of the desktop). If you plan to create part or all of the standard Macintosh interface for actual use, it's critical that every element of the Macintosh interface acts *exactly* as described in Apple's *Human Interface Guidelines: The Apple Desktop Interface.*

■ **Figure 4-3** A training stack that simulates the standard Macintosh interface

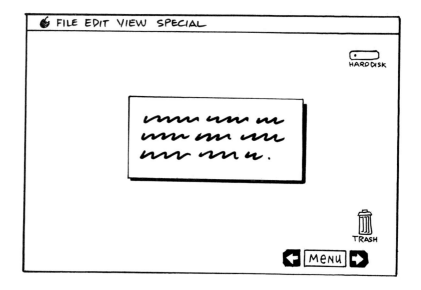

The stack shown in Figure 4-4 simulates a different piece of software, again for training purposes. Visual styles this far afield from the standard HyperCard elements give stack design an enormous flexibility and versatility. Note that in this example, more familiar HyperCard elements, such as the floating text box and the travel buttons, have been superimposed on the simulated software layout.

■ **Figure 4-4**   A stack that simulates other software for training purposes

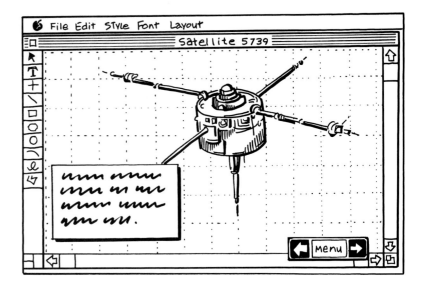

The stack shown in Figure 4-5 doesn't resemble HyperCard at all. The freedom and playfulness of this stack design show the power that different visual styles can have. The screen is essentially a blank canvas on which to design an interface and an experience for the user. Although some visual styles require more graphic expertise (and sometimes equipment) to implement, this screen demonstrates the impact that typography alone can achieve.

■ **Figure 4-5** A stack that doesn't resemble HyperCard at all

Card layout

In this section, "card layout" refers to card in its broadest sense, including both the card layer and the background layer.

It's best to design your layout after you've determined who will use your stack, the stack's subject matter, the way in which to present the subject matter, and at least a rough model for how the users will navigate through the stack.

In short, you need to know something about *what* will be on a card before you can decide *where* to place it. And where you place it can tell the user a lot about what the object is.

Common card elements are text, illustrations, other graphic elements such as borders, and both navigation and stack-usage buttons. Consistent card layout gives the user a feeling of stability and lessens the teaching required.

Try to use a standard card layout for any parts of your stack that are similar. In a real estate stack showing houses for sale, for instance, all the overview cards should have a similar layout, and all the floor-plan cards should have a similar, though perhaps not identical, layout.

Play with card layout. Perhaps you'll doodle on paper first, or perhaps you'll work directly on the screen. Most people who begin on paper end up spending most of their time on screen eventually, where it's easy to move elements around and rearrange them. Try different options. Mock up several different layouts, and test people for their reactions.

To help you design your card layout, first decide where you want each element to appear on the screen. After you know where you want the elements to appear, then decide whether they best belong in the background, because they're common to most or all cards, or whether they belong in the foreground or "card" layer.

Grids and labels

For most stacks, some kind of invisible grid layout is best. A grid layout is one in which certain areas of the screen have been blocked off for specific functions. Sometimes it's easier to figure out grid layouts first on paper (or large, screen-sized notecards), and then, after you get roughly what you want, move to working on screen.

Figure 4-6 shows various grids and the final on-screen version made from them.

■ **Figure 4-6** Different grids and their final versions

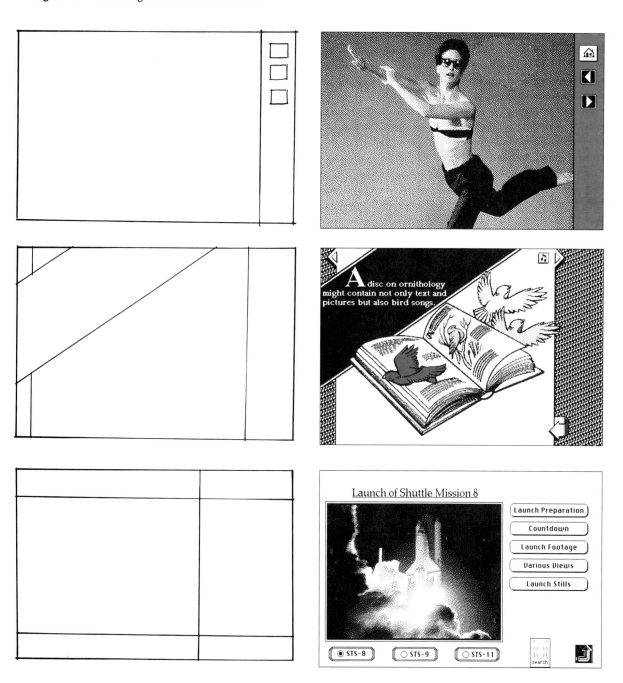

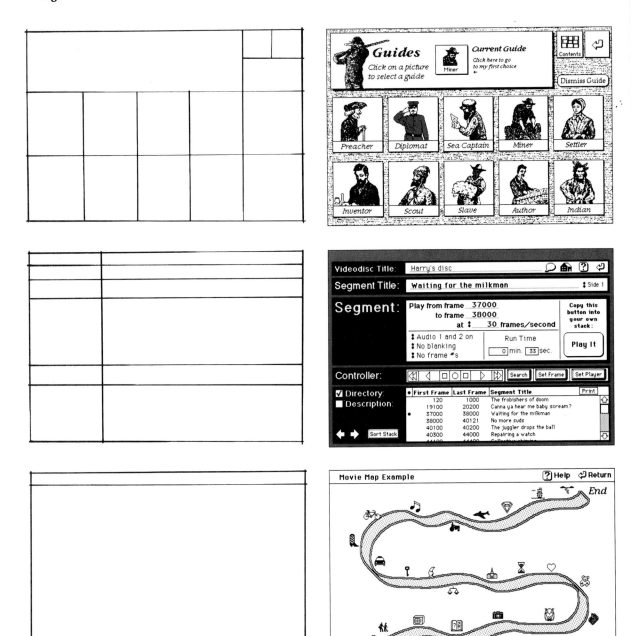

Here are some rules of thumb to keep in mind as you design your grid layout:

- Keep it simple.
- Use grids *especially* for text-only cards.
- Use size to indicate priority: make important things bigger. Give the largest grid space to the element that's the card's focus.
- Set up the grid so the user is visually led to "do the right thing."
- Make permanent buttons small and unobtrusive.
- Put permanent buttons along a card's edges and edges of grid areas within the card.
- Separate permanent navigation buttons from card-specific ones.
- Put buttons that change part of a screen next to the thing they affect.

Keep it simple

Grid layouts don't need to be complicated or to have lots of sections. A one- or two-part grid can be quite powerful. The usefulness of a grid comes from the visual ordering it gives the screen. In Figure 4-6, for instance, compare the dancer screen, with one of the simplest grids, to the videodisc controller screen, which uses one of the most complex grids. The visual impact of the dancer screen is far more striking.

Grids need not be rectangular. A grid showing perspective might have triangular areas. Other screen layouts could use circular or oval areas on the grid. Experiment.

Use grids *especially* for text-only cards

Text is hard to read on-screen. Some things that can decrease legibility even further are lines that are too long, reaching edge-to-edge across the screen; lines that are too short, breaking a sentence every one or two words; and text that fills its frame right to the edge, with no visual break. Laying text out in a grid can make the lines a readable length and give the eye some restful white space.

When several pieces of text are on the screen at once, as in Figure 4-7, it's difficult to know what to read first. Especially in the example on the left, the reader doesn't know whether to read the top chunk, since it's first in the vertical hierarchy, or the chunk that says "Title," since it's first in the informational hierarchy.

The grid used in the example on the right of Figure 4-7 clarifies the order and relationship of the elements on screen. Users appreciate structure, particularly with a design element like text for which so much tradition and convention already exists. Note that this convention changes with language. English and most European languages are read left-to-right, beginning at the upper-left corner. Some Asian and Middle Eastern languages are read top-to-bottom or right-to-left.

■ **Figure 4-7**   The grid on the right makes clear the order of the text

 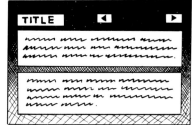

Use size to indicate priority

When people look at a stack, their eyes are drawn to the largest element on the screen. You can take advantage of this tendency by making the largest element the one you most want them to focus on. Let this guide you in your user interface decisions, too; users confronted with a large button and a small one will assume the large one is more important or more likely to be useful.

Set up the grid so the user is visually led to "do the right thing"

Not only should the items that draw the user's eye be the important ones, but the layout should also imply relationships between the items. Consider the screens in Figure 4-8; on the left, the relationship between the different buttons is confusing; the user doesn't know how to interpret the grid. On the right, the grid layout clarifies which buttons are the primary ones, and which are subordinate.

■ **Figure 4-8** The grid on the right clarifies main elements and subordinate ones

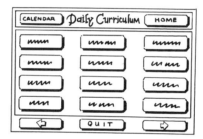 

Make permanent buttons small and unobtrusive

If you have many elements on your screen, don't obscure large portions of the screen area with permanent buttons (those that appear on every card). Large or attention-grabbing buttons take up valuable screen space.

In Figure 4-9, the permanent travel buttons in the image on the left seem to be the most important elements because of their size and strong coloring. The middle image, by contrast, shows the same elements resized and moved so that the permanent elements have receded into the periphery. The final version includes a scanned photographic image of the dancer.

■ **Figure 4-9**   Buttons that overpower, the same buttons made less obtrusive, and the final version

Put permanent buttons along the grid's edges

People can remember visual elements that are next to boundaries or borders more easily than elements that are not. Because navigation buttons are normally used on several cards, putting them near the edges will help users remember their locations. By positioning these and any other permanent buttons at the grid's edges, you free the user to focus visually on the content of the stack.

Separate permanent navigation buttons from card-specific ones

If your stack has some navigation buttons that are common to every card and other navigation buttons that change according to what card the user is on, separate these buttons. It's easier for users to identify one portion of the screen as constant and unchanging than it is for them to sort out which buttons have changed each time.

Put buttons next to the part of the card they affect

When buttons are out near the edge of a card, users expect them to affect the entire card. If a button affects only a small area of the card, move the button next to that area, so users get a visual indication of the relationship.

In Figure 4-10, the arrows in the image on the left are placed in the lower corner of the card. This seems to imply that clicking one of those arrows would result in moving to another card. The rendition in the right-hand screen clarifies that these arrows control only the displayed warrior. Clicking one of those arrows would scroll to another part of the warrior mural, not go to another card. Users would have to think harder to understand the actions of the buttons in the design on the left.

■ **Figure 4-10**   The arrows' location on the screen on the right clarifies what they control

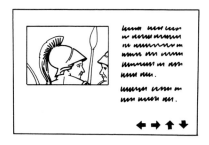 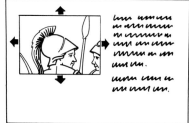

Cards and backgrounds

Cards in HyperCard consist of essentially two layers. Ordinarily the top or "card" layer is transparent, so you can see through to the "background" layer. In general, use the background layer to keep any elements that will be shared across most or all the stack's cards, and use the card layer for elements that are specific to one card or change with every card.

Elements at the background level

Decide which elements will be common to all cards in your stack—pictures, navigation buttons, and text fields—and put those in the background. If you have an item that appears on most (but not all) of the cards in a background, it may be best to put it in the background and hide it on the cards you don't want it on.

Pictures can take up a lot of memory. To save space, store a picture in the background and hide it on cards that don't need it, instead of repeating the same picture several times on the card layer.

■ To hide a background *picture,* select the area of the card (from the card, not the background) you want to be opaque, and choose Opaque from the Paint menu.

■ To hide a background *button,* select the button you want to hide. Then copy the button, which will place an identical button on top of the original one. Now make the new button opaque but empty.

■ To hide a background *field,* simply don't put text in it, if it's transparent, or cover it with an opaque, locked card field or an opaque button.

A stack using different backgrounds, such as a catalog stack showing office furniture on one background and home furniture on another, should have a consistent graphic look on every background—the same pixel widths for lines, the same styles of illustrations, the same set of icons, and the same kinds of fonts. This strategy will keep your stack's look consistent and provide a stable context for the users, minimizing their learning time. However, the backgrounds for different sections should be quickly differentiable, so as not to confuse either you or your users.

Keep the design simple. When you design the background for a stack, it may look very bare. When you add the information to the stack, it will look much more intricate. If a lot of the information is common to every card, however, your background will probably be more complicated.

Elements at the card level

After you've put all shared elements in the background layer, everything remaining goes in the foreground "card" level. These are items that change with each card, or are only shared by a few cards, such as text, illustrations, and card-specific buttons.

Users often focus on the card elements, but the background elements give the stack its distinctive look, because they form a context for the card elements.

In Figure 4-11, you can see three very different ways of distributing visual information across the card "foreground" and the background. In the cash register example, almost all the information on the screen is in the background; only the tutorial information itself changes from screen to screen.

In the bar chart example, the background has only two elements—the black background bar and the cross-hatch perspective grid—but they provide most of the visual power in the screen.

The third example is almost the opposite of the first one. In the bicycle repair screen, most of the information is in the card layer, with only the three frames in the background.

Your stack's specific needs will dictate which elements you put on which layer. These three examples are included to give you an idea of situations in which you might want to put information primarily in one layer or the other.

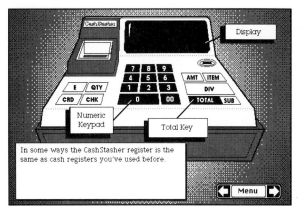
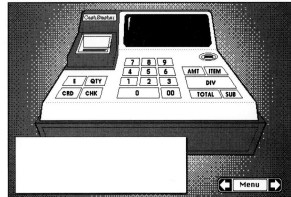

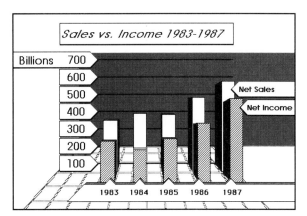
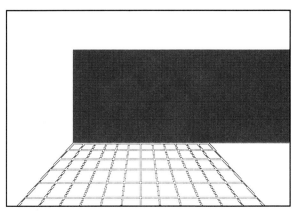

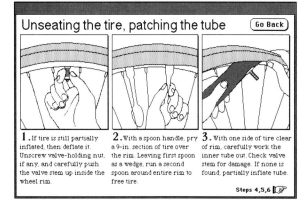
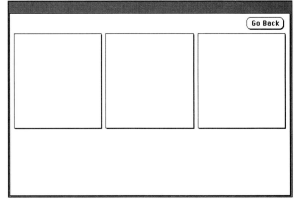

Copying cards

One of the easiest ways to build stacks is to copy cards, modify them, and paste them or their elements somewhere else. This is especially easy because HyperCard pastes a copied element in exactly the same place as it was on the original card. This means you can very quickly put a card button, a graphic, or a text field in the same place on a number of cards just by copying it once and then doing the paste command on other cards, even if those cards are in different stacks.

When you copy an entire card, however, you also copy its background. If your stack has more than one background and you unwittingly paste a card with background A into a group of cards with background B, you can run into these problems:

- If you create new cards immediately following the inserted card, they will have that card's background, which may not be what you intend.

- If you change background A, thinking you're changing the whole section, the cards with background B won't change.

One way to keep similar backgrounds straight is to give them unique names. Then you can always check the name to make sure you have the background you intend.

Illustrations

Illustrations are the pictures that appear in stacks, whereas *graphics* or *visual design* refer to all visual elements. Not every stack uses illustrations; some rely only on good card layout to tie the components together. But HyperCard is a visual medium, and illustrations are a way of using HyperCard's power.

Illustrations can enrich your design and illuminate your points. You can weave the text and illustrations together, each doing its own job, so that they form an integrated unit. A complex illustration with a simple text box can often convey as much information as a long text box alone.

The screens in Figure 4-12 show the power of even a small graphic to cut down the required text. In the screen on the left, it takes several lines of text to describe the Play Sound button. The screen on the right conveys precisely the same information, but, like in good advertisements, the text and graphics work together to provide the information.

■ **Figure 4-12** The screen on the right uses a simple graphic to reduce the text needed

Sometimes a simple graphic is insufficient, and a full illustration is needed. The screens in Figure 4-13 contain the same information about bones and arches of the human foot. The left screen describes all the components in meticulous detail. The screen on the right uses medical illustration to convey the information.

■ **Figure 4-13** The screen on the right uses an illustration to reduce the text needed

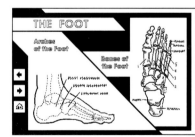

When you're using illustrations that seem to pop up and cover part of the card, as with the `show card picture` command, don't hide essential buttons or text. The example in Figure 4-14 shows a common design oversight: when the detailed picture pops up, it covers all the navigation buttons, so the user can't leave the card without first closing the picture. The design on the right keeps the permanent buttons available to the user at all times.

■ **Figure 4-14** The pop-up illustration on the left covers the buttons; the one on the right does not

Choose illustrations that match your stack's graphic look. For example, a medical stack might use high-quality line drawings or photographic-quality art. A game stack might use cartoon imagery. Be certain that the imagery you choose fits the audience, subject matter, and purpose of your stack. Ask reviewers what the visual style conveys to them.

When choosing images for illustrations, try to avoid possible nationalist, racist, or sexist overtones, or other cultural biases that could detract from your stack's purpose by offending some users. Again, ask reviewers' opinions.

Scanned images

Scanned or digitized images look like photographs on screen. You could scan a drawing or photograph of your hand, for instance, or you could scan the hand itself. By using a scanner or digitizer, you can produce screen images more quickly and in a wider range of visual styles than you can by using on-screen tools.

A flatbed scanner works like a copy machine: You hook the scanner to your Macintosh and load the scanner software. You can then put paper or objects on the scanner and have the digitized, photographic image appear on screen. If you use the HyperScan software that comes with the Apple Scanner, your scanned image will appear in a HyperCard stack, ready for pasting to your own stack.

A video digitizer, shown in the margin, works on the same principles, except that instead of copying from the bed of a scanner, you can capture any images that your video camera is pointing at. Generally, the video camera is hooked to a hardware digitizer box that in turn hooks to the Macintosh, which is running special scanner software.

Scanners are currently the fastest, easiest way to produce high-quality photographic or freehand illustrations for stacks. The primary drawback to scanners is the potential for legal problems. Most images in the world belong to someone. The surest way to avoid lawsuits is to create your own imagery and scan it, rather than scanning imagery without legal permission. Many people who own imagery, however, willingly give permission for its use. If you do want to use someone else's images, ask their permission and see your lawyer for advice.

It's often faster for illustrators to draw on paper by hand, scan the images in, and clean them up, than it is to work on the screen from scratch. Also, this method can give your stacks a wider and freer variety of styles.

The dancer stack illustrations in Figures 4-6 and 4-9 were both scanned using a flatbed like the Apple Scanner shown in the margin, as was the initial salmon image in Figure 4-1. Figure 4-15 shows another example of a scanned illustration.

The examples in Figure 4-15 show the three steps of the scanning process. In the first frame, on the left, the illustrator has drawn the Porsche on paper. The second frame shows that same hand-drawing, after it's been scanned into the computer. The final frame, on the right, shows the final screen after the text and navigational elements have been added to the scanned image.

■ **Figure 4-15** A hand-drawn illustration, its scanned image, and the final screen

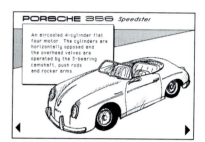

Typography

Typography refers to the visual appearance of text on screen. Writing is discussed in Chapter 6, but text placement and appearance need to be considered as graphic elements when doing your screen layout.

Text in a stack can come from several sources:

- It can be typed by you, the author, as either regular text in a field or as Paint text. You may want to "lock" regular text, as described below.

- It can be typed by the user into a text field. (Don't lock user text fields in which you want users to type.)

- As Paint text, it can be imported using the Import Paint command from the File menu.

Fonts

Fonts have a big impact on the look of your stack. Some fonts, such as Geneva and Helvetica, have a clean, modern look; other fonts, like New York and Times, are more classic; Courier looks like typewritten text.

In general, you should only use one or two fonts, using different sizes and styles for emphasis. Multiple fonts can muddy the contrast and confuse users. Some fonts, such as Geneva, New York, and Chicago, look better on the screen; others, such as Helvetica, Times, and Palatino, were designed to print well on a particular printer.

If your stack contains text that you don't want the user to change, you can lock the text from the Field Info dialog box (check "Lock Text"). Or, you can lock an individual card or background (check "Can't modify" or "Can't delete" in the Card Info or Background Info dialog box). Locked text can't be edited. The Browse tool, ordinarily shaped like a hand, won't change to the I-beam, text-insertion pointer over locked text, so users won't be able to select or type anything.

Keep text legible

Avoid using only capital letters, except for a word or two of emphasis or for short titles or buttons. It's much easier for people to read a mix of uppercase and lowercase letters. Plain text is more legible than italicized text. Lines of text that are too long, reaching edge-to-edge across the screen, or too short, breaking sentences every one or two words, are difficult to read. If you are using a small font size (which is not recommended because it's usually hard to read), make the line width shorter.

Use standard fonts or provide fonts

If possible, use the standard fonts included on the HyperCard disks for all the text fields in your stacks. If you use a font that your users don't have, another font will be substituted and may look bad or not fit in the space you designed.

If you need to use a nonstandard font for text fields, you should either install it into your stack itself, or include it as a separate font resource and instruct users to install it into their System file with the Font/DA Mover utility. Installing a font into your stack ensures that it will always be available, but it takes up disk space. If it's a fairly common font, users may already have it; include it as a separate file for those who don't, along with instructions.

Table 4-1 lists the standard fonts and sizes that come with Macintosh System files.

■ **Table 4-1** Standard fonts included in System files

Fonts	Sizes available
Chicago	12
Courier	10, 12
Geneva	9, 10, 12, 14, 18
Helvetica	10, 12
Monaco	9
New York	9, 10, 12, 14, 18
Times	10, 12, 18*

*(Times 18 is in HyperCard itself, not the System file.)

If you are using Paint text instead of field text, as described below, you can use any font. With Paint text, HyperCard saves the exact bitmapped image of the font, so all users see the same thing, no matter which fonts they have.

Choosing Paint text or field text

If you or the user will ever want to change the text, use field text (regular text). You can edit the text, move the field around, or change the font, size, or attributes for an entire field at a time. Searching can be done only on field text, which means that localizing for international markets is much easier with field text. Field text will look smoother than Paint text when printed on a LaserWriter® printer, but the word-wraps and spacing may change from what you see on screen.

If you know what you want to say, don't need to change the text much, don't need it to be searchable, don't need to localize it for international markets, don't need it to print without jagged edges on a LaserWriter, or don't think your users will have the font you're using (and you don't want to provide the font), use Paint text.

Paint text can be manipulated graphically—you can invert it or flip it, design elaborate initial letters, or fill it with patterns. It's essentially graphics that are letters. To produce Paint text, choose the Paint Text tool (which looks like a capital letter A). If you want to transform existing field text into Paint text, copy the field text, select the Paint Text tool, and then paste. Or, use Export Paint/Import Paint from the File menu.

Visual effects

Visual effects can work powerfully for you or just as powerfully against you. The best rule of thumb for choosing visual effects is *be consistent.* If you always use the same visual effect to open the menu, people will come to associate the effect with the action.

Be unobtrusive. Just as you wouldn't want to use twenty different fonts on one card, don't use twenty different visual effects to go through a stack. Make your visual effects work to support the metaphor or navigation method you've chosen.

Remember that visual effects won't work if you're looking at a stack on a monitor set for color. If your visual effects are crucial to the meaning or operation of your stack, include a warning to users that they must have the monitor set to black and white. You could include a test: set up a striking visual effect, such as

```
visual effect dissolve to black
visual effect dissolve to card
```

and ask if they've seen it. If they haven't, tell them how to go to the Control Panel and switch Monitors from color to black-and-white with two grays.

When you begin studying how to use visual effects, start watching television and movies with an analytic eye. The visual effects in HyperCard are all found in these screen media. Observe how often directors simply "cut" to another screen, using no visual effect at all. Watch the difference in connotation when they instead dissolve or zoom to the next scene.

Visual effects can be your ally because of what they connote. A simple cut to the next card, with no visual effect, connotes efficiency. The transition is either simple or unimportant.

The illustrations in the margin represent the different visual effects. In each case, the visual effect occurs as a transition between the initial "Fun" screen and the final screen picturing balloons.

■ **Figure 4-16**   The initial screen on which the visual effect will occur, and the final screen

 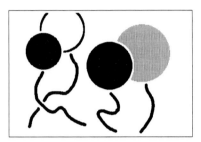

Dissolve

Iris open

Dissolve, one of the most frequently used effects, conveys a purposeful slowing as if the transition itself were important, or the two cards sufficiently different that the user needs time to adjust.

Iris open and iris close connote zooming in and out or information popping up. They can give a feeling of depth, as if the user were going into or backing out of three-dimensional space. They're good for focusing on one piece of the screen and expanding it.

Zoom

Wipe left

Scroll left

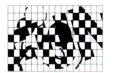

Checkerboard

Venetian blinds

Barn door open

Note that there are two differences between zoom and iris. **Zoom** gives the illusion of zooming by drawing successive white rectangles on top of the image, whereas iris actually opens or closes to reveal the new image. The zoom open effect starts from the spot on the screen you clicked, but iris always opens from the center. You can cause a zoom to begin at any point on the screen by having the button that the user clicks send a message to another button on the screen, which, in turn, handles the zoom open script. Zoom close, though, will always close to the center of the screen.

Wipe left can give the impression of turning a page, because it reveals the next card as if that next card were underneath the first one. **Scroll** left, a similar effect, differs in that the next card does not seem to be underneath, but instead appears to be slid into view from the right, as the original card slides out of view to the left.

Wipe and scroll left give a sense of moving forward in the stack; wipe and scroll right convey moving backward. Wipe and scroll up and down give the impression of flipping through cards, index style. These effects provide kinesthetic reminders to users, and help users orient themselves within a stack.

Checkerboard and **venetian blinds** are loud, flashy visual effects, that connote "Now, for something completely different . . ." If an effect calls undue attention to itself in your stack, it's best not to use it; however, these effects are good choices for showing a visible break or a sense of simultaneous timing.

Barn door open gives the impression of opening a stage, opening a play, or opening a window onto something else. Unlike iris open, barn door open doesn't connote that the thing being opened is smaller or is in need of greater magnification. Barn door close has the effect of closing a scene, being finished, or going back to an entry point.

If you're not sure about your visual effects, ask about them in your testing. Ask the users to tell you which visual effects felt obtrusive or "wrong."

Animation

Animation, the illusion of movement, has a big impact on users. But because of their exposure to movies and television, users have high expectations of animation quality.

Animation is an effective way to open stacks, to illustrate movement within stacks—as in simulating other software or user motions—or to announce the beginning of another section of the stack. Animation can be used to entertain and to inform. Be clear why you're using it.

Let your users control when animation begins. Even in the very beginning, when your stack has just opened and you're tempted to give a flashy animated show, stop. Plan the whole flashy show, and even start the stack with a little cyclic animation, but give the user two buttons: "Begin" and "Skip to main menu," for instance. This gets users doing something early, and it gives them the option of seeing the animation or not, as they choose. (If no one will use this stack more than once, just provide the "Begin" button.)

If you are writing a stack to run on several kinds of machines, be prepared to spend time fine-tuning your animation. Something that looks great on a Macintosh II can run too slowly for comfort on a Macintosh Plus. If it must run on both extremes, it's best to time it so it looks acceptable on the Macintosh Plus, then use the `wait` command and tick values to slow it down on the Mac II. It can still run faster on the Mac II, if you wish, but this way the speed is under your control.

Animation can be achieved in HyperCard by eight different methods, each with its own advantages and drawbacks. From simplest to most complex, here are the eight ways:

- Flip from card to card rapidly, in sequence.
- Use visual effects to provide transitions.
- Hide and show pictures, buttons, or fields.
- Use Paint tools to draw or manipulate the images in real time.
- Use custom or stock HyperCard button icons as animation "sprites."
- Create custom fonts that look like images, not letters.
- Write XMCDs in Pascal or C to do the animation.
- Exit HyperCard to an animation application.

Flipping from card to card is one of the simplest ways to produce animation. It's quick to produce and has the advantage of printing well, so that reviewers who need to see the animation can see a rendering of it on paper as well as on screen. The printout is useful for soliciting written feedback on particular frames or sequencing issues. This method is expensive, though, both in the memory it requires and in the relatively slow performance time it delivers.

Visual effects provide a limited amount of animation that's readily available. Animated wipes, scrolls, venetian blinds, and checkerboards, for instance, are available with one short command. These animations require very little memory or scripting skill, but have the disadvantage of not showing up on a printout.

Using `hide` or `show` commands to reveal a picture, button, or field can be fairly simple. You have many options, all of which run quickly. It can be difficult to edit your animations, however, and these methods don't print well. You may spend more time trying to produce printed copies than you did designing the animation.

Paint tools can be directed by HyperCard scripts to draw or manipulate images in real time. This technique requires little memory to operate. However, if the animation is halted by Command-period, it may not work correctly thereafter. Be sure to test this animation carefully.

Both custom and stock HyperCard button icons can serve as animation **sprites,** small figures that make up the various stages of one animated motion. You could animate talking, for instance, by making two buttons, one for a closed mouth and one for an open mouth, and then hiding and showing them in rapid succession. This method provides excellent performance and needs little memory, but limits you to the relatively small size of a button. In addition, creating the buttons can be tedious and the custom icons don't always copy and paste well.

Custom fonts take advantage of the Macintosh computer's speed in displaying and manipulating characters. If you were to animate talking by this method, you could make a "letter" that looked like an open mouth, and have this letter appear whenever the *A* key was pressed. By displaying this image in a text field in real time, you can get an animation that runs quickly and is extremely easy to script and change. Building the custom font characters, however, is difficult and time-consuming, and it's hard to print a representation of the animation.

You can write custom programs, called **XCMDs,** in either C or Pascal, and call these from within HyperCard. Because of the power of the languages used, XCMDs allow you to extend the animation capabilities of HyperCard, and the resulting animations run swiftly. Writing the XCMDs requires programming skill, however, and altering the animations can require editing those programs.

Your final option is to write scripts that open other applications, such as any of the commercially available animation packages, and then return to HyperCard when the animation is finished. But while that animation is running, HyperCard has no control and is inaccessible. In addition, you must supply the user with not only your stack, but the animation application as well.

Summary

HyperCard is a visual medium. Graphic elements such as visual style, card layout, metaphor, illustrations, typography, visual effects, and animation are an integral part of any stack. They are especially powerful in communicating the stack's environment and its navigation.

A visual metaphor, such as a television set, can make complex navigation choices seem simple. Clean card layout frees the user to focus on the stack's content. An integrated visual style, in which illustrations, typography, and animation convey a single message, reinforces the purpose of the stack.

Many of the problems revealed in user testing can be solved by effective graphic design. Sometimes the solution is as simple as changing the card's grid, separating permanent buttons from card-specific ones, or moving related elements closer to each other on the screen.

The graphic look of your stack can be as simple or as complex as you wish. With new tools, such as scanners and digitizers, you no longer need artistic or programming expertise to produce stacks of photographic quality. But simple, spare graphics that convey your message without ostentation can be just as effective.

Buttons

BUTTONS LET USERS INTERACT WITH AND MOVE AROUND WITHIN A STACK. Buttons are the main means by which users can control what a stack does for them. Buttons are also used as a general-purpose tool by HyperTalk scripters to provide stack functionality. In this chapter, the focus is on buttons whose purpose is to allow users to control the actions in a stack.

Buttons that allow users to move through a stack are called "navigation" or "travel" buttons to differentiate them from buttons that let users interact with the stack.

Make it clear where buttons are and what they do. It's best if the user can get this information simply by looking at the button. The button's appearance, placement, and grouping with other buttons work together to convey this information.

Make it clear what screen elements are buttons. Test this critical feature with your pilot users: can people find the buttons on your screens? Are they aware that the buttons exist? Do they select buttons correctly the first time, or do they find the buttons confusing?

Figure 5-1 shows an example screen in three different phases of development. In the left screen, the buttons are not visually apparent, and the user has little hope of finding them. The middle screen is an improvement, since the user can now find the buttons, but they disrupt the text's readability.

The screen on the right shows a solution in which the buttons are obvious and visually invite the user to make a choice. This third screen also makes the Commands and Functions buttons bigger and separate from the Main Menu button, so the user realizes it's a different kind of button and is unlikely to make the mistake of selecting Main Menu as a response.

■ **Figure 5-1** Buttons that are not obvious, then obvious but disruptive, then clear and distinguishable

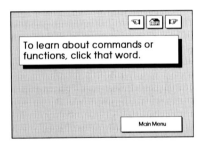 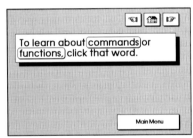 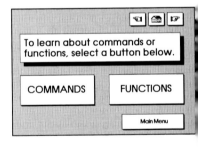

Feedback

The effect of "Auto hilite"

Users need feedback to reassure them that they have really clicked the button. They expect this kind of feedback from their other Macintosh experience. A simple and familiar way to provide it is to have the button image invert (become highlighted) when the user clicks it. For buttons whose outlines are visible, develop the habit of checking "Auto hilite" in the Button Info dialog box when you make a new button. This action automatically implements button highlighting.

Buttons that are transparent, though, with a picture behind them, usually don't look good if they are graphically highlighted, because the rectangle of the button may have no relation to the image's edges. To provide feedback in these cases, you may wish to provide audible feedback or tie a distinctive visual effect to the button. The examples shown in Figures 5-2 through 5-5 illustrate different ways of providing feedback with transparent buttons and the effect of those different methods.

■ **Figure 5-2** A transparent button covering a picture

■ **Figure 5-3**   When highlighted, this transparent button's appearance is jarring

■ **Figure 5-4**   Sound is another way to provide feedback

- **Figure 5-5**   Moving momentarily to another card with an inverted image can simulate highlighting

The solution shown in Figure 5-5 is to simulate highlighting by going to a card that's a duplicate of the first card except for the inverted image. The button script would specify going to this card on `mouseDown`; the `mouseUp` handler then would perform whatever function the button is assigned.

When the button is instead a standard, visible shape such as a rounded rectangle, a shadowed rectangle, or one of the standard HyperCard button icons, feedback is simpler to implement: just choose "Auto hilite" in the Button Info dialog box when creating the button. In addition, you can provide audio feedback to reinforce or supplement the visual highlighting.

Button placement

If buttons are near each other on the screen, users will assume they are related. You can use this assumption to your advantage by grouping your buttons functionally on a card. You might, for instance, put buttons common to every card in one place, and buttons that change with each card in another. Or, you might put all buttons associated with an illustration near that illustration. Figure 4-10 in the previous chapter, with the four arrows near the picture of the warrior, showed the power of locating the buttons near the region they control.

Be sure the travel buttons remain visible and accessible, no matter what users do on the card. If your stack lets users produce pop-up graphics or pop-up fields, for instance, make sure the images don't hide the travel buttons. Figure 4-14 in the previous chapter showed an example of travel buttons being hidden by the vase's detailed pop-up picture.

Buttons on cards and backgrounds

You can put a button on either the card or the background. Which option you choose depends mainly on how widely used the button is.

The background is best for buttons that will be on most or all cards. Arrow buttons or other standard traveling icons are often put in the background. To obscure a button on the few exceptions, in this case, create a blank, opaque *card* button with an empty script over the button and picture you want hidden.

The card layer is best for buttons that are card-specific, such as check boxes and radio buttons that have different settings on each card. If these buttons are in the background, the same setting will show up every time the button appears.

Standard arrow buttons

Custom arrow buttons

Arrow buttons

Many stacks use arrow buttons as one of the primary ways for users to move around. Arrow buttons are usually icon buttons, although they don't have to be—they could be transparent buttons over custom graphics.

Point your arrows in a direction that's appropriate to your stack. In a stack using a book metaphor, for instance, the arrows should point sideways because that's how pages turn. In a stack using a map, the arrows should go up and down for north and south, right and left for east and west.

Select a visual effect that matches your arrow. A right-pointing arrow should appear to move your user to the right (by using a scroll or wipe *left*). This helps users orient themselves and is an easy way to reinforce your navigational structure. The following figures illustrate ways to use arrows.

■ **Figure 5-6** Arrows that suit the page-turning metaphor

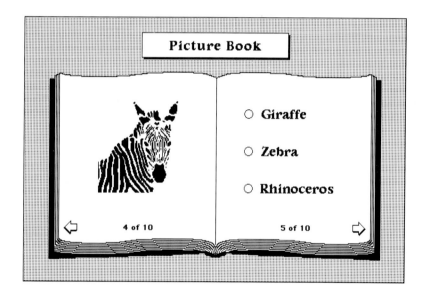

■ **Figure 5-7**   Arrows that suit the rotation metaphor

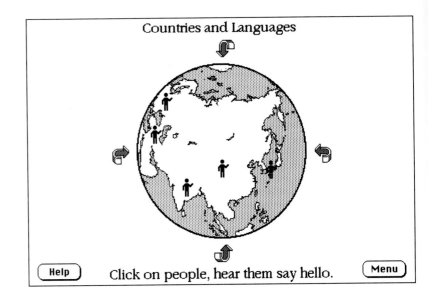

■ **Figure 5-8**   Arrows that suit the zooming metaphor

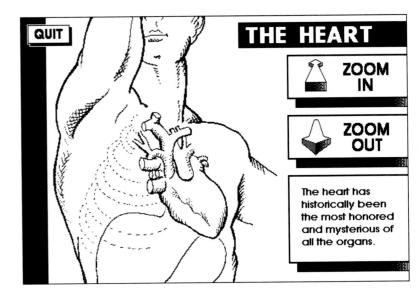

The arrows in Figures 5-6 through 5-8, by visually matching the action they perform, provide a powerful navigation message to the user. The rotational arrows in Figure 5-7, for instance, give the user an immediate message that navigation will proceed around the globe, without any text or additional design elements required. Not only do the buttons suit and support the metaphor of each stack, but they also match the visual style of the screen.

Be meticulous with your arrows and provide only the options that make sense. The first card in a stack, for instance, should have a forward arrow, but shouldn't have a backward one. (If you have a backward arrow in the background, cover it up.) In other places, you may want to show both buttons to remind the user these traveling options are usually available, but show one of them dimmed to indicate it doesn't work on this particular card.

It's usually best to keep the arrow buttons in the same place on every card, so users who want to move quickly through don't have to stop and look for the arrow. If you have arrows associated with a specific part of the card instead of overall navigation, put them near the part they affect.

The arrows in Figure 5-7, for instance, are next to the globe they affect, whereas the arrows in Figure 5-8 are on the edge of the card, since they affect the entire card image. Even the page-turning arrows in Figure 5-6 are located on the picture book, whose pages they turn, and not on the larger card itself.

Although arrows are a small visual part of most screens, they are a large part of the user's experience because they are one of the most frequently used elements. People make strong assumptions about the stack's navigation without realizing it, and sometimes changing the look and placement of arrows can solve major navigational confusion on the part of the users.

Icon buttons

Icon buttons have pictures (icons) as part of the button itself. The pictures are 32-by-32-pixel drawings that stay with the button as you move it around. You can get icons easily by clicking the Icon button in the Button Info dialog box and then clicking the icon you want from the icons dialog box. Another way to get an icon is simply to copy a button from the Button Ideas stack and paste it into your stack. When you copy the entire button, you also copy a prewritten script, which is not the case if you choose the icon alone. Or, you can make custom buttons yourself in MacPaint, and then transfer them into a commercially available resource editor such as IconMaker™ . The 32-by-32-pixel graphic limitation makes it easier to do stylized icon buttons than realistic ones.

Icon buttons are useful when

- you want a picture associated with a button's function

- you want the picture to remain with the button, even when you move the button around

- the button is used in several places

- the button can be stylized or otherwise graphically rendered within a 32-by-32-bit limitation

■ **Figure 5-9** Standard HyperCard button icons

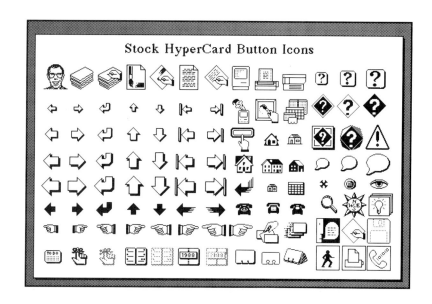

■ **Figure 5-10** Some custom buttons

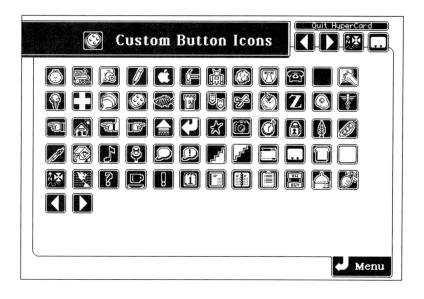

Icon buttons are not a good choice if you need rich graphic detail or a large picture. If you need the button on only one card, you can give up the handiness of the picture remaining with the button in favor of more graphic richness. In these cases, you may instead want to use a transparent button over a card or background picture.

Some of the standard button icons available through the icons dialog box have widely understood common uses. The return-arrow icon, for example, which points down, then curves to the left, is used to mean "Go back to the most recent decision point." In a stack about realty, for instance, the user might choose Residential Properties from the main menu, and go to a section of cards describing different homes. Clicking the forward and backward arrows would show other residences; clicking the return-arrow button would return the user to the main menu.

The icons that look like small houses mean "Go to HyperCard's Home card."

The icon that looks like a cartoon speech balloon is used to mean, "Provide information about this stack's purpose and its authors" (shown in an "About" box).

Icons are meant to give a graphic idea of a button's function. When you copy an icon button, you get its script as well. If you copy only the icon for your own button, it's best to use the button for a purpose similar to the icon's message. Above all, don't give the button a function contrary to what users expect.

Transparent buttons

Transparent buttons are useful in several cases:

- over a word in a locked, nonscrolling text field, especially if that word is clearly designated as a button or when you want to make the text appear to be highlighted

- over part of a picture, when a visible button would get in the way of the picture

- over a small picture or icon-like picture that appears in only one place

- over a small picture or icon-like picture if you want a pictorial button but don't have a resource maker, or for some reason don't want to create a real icon button

- over a picture that is too large to fit in an icon

Generally, the "Auto hilite" option doesn't work well with transparent buttons unless they are aligned precisely with a rectangular picture, or aligned over text to look like standard text highlighting. There are other ways of providing user feedback, though; see "Feedback" earlier in this chapter for more details.

Remember, when you cut and paste or move transparent buttons, you'll affect only the button and its script, not the picture or text it appeared over. If you want to hide a transparent button and its associated graphic, create an opaque but empty card button over the button you want hidden.

Named buttons

There's a saying that "a picture is worth a thousand words." In creating user interfaces, there are also times when a word is worth a thousand pictures, or times when a picture and a word are worth about five hundred each, and you need both.

Named buttons, which you get by checking "Show name" in the Button Info dialog box, provide their own reference information. It's useful to choose named buttons when you want to save space in your text fields, or when an icon would be too ambiguous, as might be the case with a return arrow in a multilayered stack.

When used in a stack that also uses icon buttons, named buttons can give you an additional way to group buttons functionally. You might decide, for instance, to use icon buttons for permanent buttons but named buttons for the card-specific ones.

Named buttons may not be a good idea if your screen is already text-intensive or if you're trying to unclutter a busy screen. They are a good choice for international stacks because translators can change the names of buttons easily. (See Appendix A for more details.)

There are other times when you'll want both a picture and a name to convey meaning. This is often true for the main menus of stacks, which address a mixture of novices, who need the words, and experienced users, who prefer the speed of pictorial clues.

In Figure 5-11, there are three different kinds of buttons on the screen: those that select automotive system, those that select kind of car, and those that let the user navigate through the stack. The example on the left has differentiated buttons by the location, but all the buttons look visually similar. The example on the right strengthens the button differences by showing each kind of button in its own visual style.

■ **Figure 5-11** In the figure on the right, different kinds of buttons have different visual styles

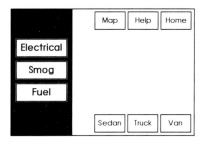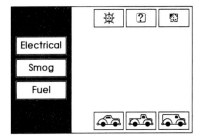

Check boxes and radio buttons

Check boxes and radio buttons are part of the standard Macintosh user interface, which users expect to act in the usual manner.

■ Do use check boxes and radio buttons for setting values or properties of something.

■ Don't use check boxes or radio buttons to travel to other cards or perform actions.

Check boxes are simple toggle switches that can be either on or off; they can appear singly or in groups, but they operate independently of each other. A user may select one, all, or none of a group of check boxes.

Check boxes are useful for times when you want your user to make several selections or decisions at once. They visually invite user interaction, especially if coupled with the pointing hand Browse tool, and often are used for quizzes. They also provide a way to indicate progress. You might want your script to check off sections on the main menu, as the user visited them, for instance.

Radio buttons, in contrast, are meant to be mutually exclusive sets. Like the buttons on a car radio, only one can be on at any time; pressing another one turns off the one that's on.

If the user must make only one choice or must always have a default selection, radio buttons are appropriate. One radio button must always be on.

Radio buttons require some scripting, however, to work properly. They do not exist ready-made anywhere, with the scripts already built in.

The examples in Figure 5-12 show the correct use of both check boxes and radio buttons.

■ **Figure 5-12**   Correct use of check boxes and radio buttons

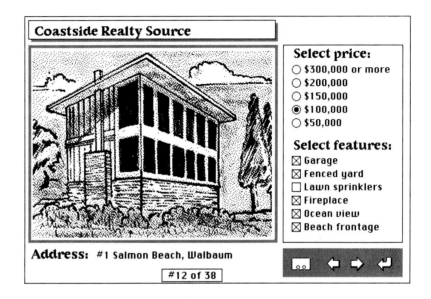

Messages to users

The methods discussed in this section, namely the Message box, "Ask" dialog boxes, and "Answer-with" dialog boxes, are not buttons. They are included here because they provide another way to interact with users.

One of the basic principles of the Macintosh interface is that the user, not the system, is always in control. Prompting the user to do something is generally against this principle, but there are some situations where you need more information from the user, such as when something is about to be deleted forever. Consider carefully whether you need to ask or tell the user something, or whether there's a way to deal with the problem that leaves the user in control.

The Message box is not appropriate for giving the users information or prompting them to do something. The Message box is only for users to enter HyperTalk commands (such as `find` "*string*" or `go to stack` "*stack name*"). Instead, use the "Ask" and "Answer-with" dialog boxes to communicate with the user.

"Ask" and "Answer-with" dialog boxes are standard, built-in ways for you to communicate with the user. You can display either one from a script by using the `ask` and `answer` commands.

"Ask" boxes let the user type a string of characters and click an OK or Cancel button, with OK being the default. Use an "Ask" box when you need the user to provide a value or type a name.

If you need a quick answer or a confirmation to continue with a time-consuming task, or you simply need to make the user aware of something, you can use an "Answer-with" dialog box. "Answer-with" dialog boxes can have one to three buttons with names that you specify; the last one in the list will be the default button. If you don't specify a "with" clause, an OK button is provided.

Summary

Buttons allow users to interact with a stack and to move within it. Users rely on buttons to provide constant information, access, and feedback as they move about a stack.

Buttons that are easily identifiable and whose function is clear allow the user to navigate and operate the stack with confidence. New users may need to be told explicitly what a button is, does, and looks like.

Some buttons, such as right and left arrows, return arrow, About box balloon, check box, radio buttons, and the house icon, have standard accepted uses. Any button in one of these shapes must conform to the expected use, or users will be confused.

Buttons can be represented by words, pictures, or both. You can create icon buttons, named buttons, or transparent buttons covering text, graphics, or both. These options let you tailor buttons extensively to meet your stack's needs.

Because buttons are the user's primary means of controlling the stack, they must be easy to locate, learn, remember, and use.

Text and Fields

TEXT REFERS TO THE VERBAL INFORMATION IN YOUR STACKS. YOU NEED TO decide what the text should say and how it should work with graphics and sound to be most effective on the screen. The text's content is a separate issue from its graphic appearance. To decide how your text should look, what fonts to use, and whether to use field text or Paint text, read the "Typography" section of Chapter 4.

Writing for the screen

Writing for the screen differs in some ways from writing for paper. Clear, concise writing is still desirable, but how the writing works with the visual and audio design is different.

Brevity

Make your writing as brief as possible. There are four ways to do this:

- Cut out unnecessary words.
- Use spaces, bullets, and card layout to make reading easier.
- Let graphics convey meaning.
- Let sound convey meaning.

Cut out unnecessary words

Write in plain and simple language. To be readable, on-screen text generally needs to be in a larger font than print text, which means there's not room for many words. A screen is smaller than a page, too, which limits the writing space further.

Figure 6-1 shows the power of brief description. The wordy version on the left has not only consumed the user's time, but also has used most of the screen space available.

- **Figure 6-1**   The text on the right is concise and readable

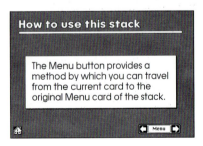 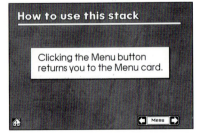

Use spaces, bullets, and card layout to make reading easier

It's easier to read text that has white space surrounding it and that doesn't reach from one side of the screen to the other. Use white space, bullets, and layout to break up the text and make it more readable.

Figure 6-2 shows two versions of a screen with identical text. But the layout and bullets make the card on the right more readable. Because of the flicker and eyestrain associated with on-line reading, this kind of size, spacing, and layout is more critical on screen than on paper.

■ **Figure 6-2**   White space and bullets make text on the right more readable

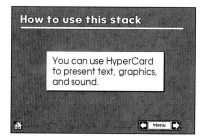 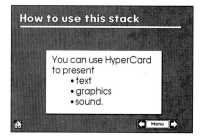

Let graphics convey meaning

Use graphics to take the burden off the words. Instead of using text to describe where things are, as in "Click the button in the lower-left corner of the screen," use graphics, such as "Click this button," with a callout pointing to the intended one. The "Illustrations" section of Chapter 4 shows some other examples of this principle.

Let sound convey meaning

Sound can convey navigation meaning—for example, "Click to continue whenever you hear this chime." Or, it can convey content meaning, as in a diagnostic stack that says, "If you hear this sound when you start your car, check your battery." Don't rely solely on sound, however, to convey vital information. See Chapter 7 for a discussion of sound in stacks.

Graceful flow

Make your words flow within screens and across screens to give users a sense of continuity and stability.

Make your screens independent of each other

Users see each screen independently, and you may not be able to tell which screens they have seen just previously. The explanatory text on your screens must be able to stand on its own, screen by screen, without untraceable references to previous screens.

The screen on the left in Figure 6-3 is not independent, since the user can't tell what "that option" is. Presumably "that option" was mentioned on a previous screen, but a user who doesn't remember what it was will feel frustrated and will have to go backward. The text on the right doesn't rely on previous screens; the user knows what to do by reading this screen only.

■ **Figure 6-3**   The text on the right can stand alone

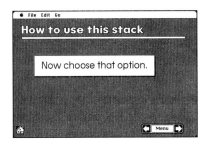
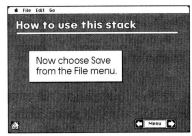

Write so that it's pleasing to the eye

Make your text readable: large, bold, well-placed. Choose a font that looks good on screen, not muddy, thin, broken, or small. Correct all grammatical and typographical errors.

Write so that it's pleasing to the ear

Write so that sentences don't sound awkward within a screen or as the user goes from screen to screen. Sometimes you won't be able to catch this flaw unless you read the text aloud to yourself or to someone else. Hear your words as a new user would hear them.

If your stack includes audio speech, make sure that the text is clear and has an easy flow when read aloud. If speech is used to augment written text, make sure they match exactly.

Interactivity

The screen is not a book. Let users interact and let them know your ground rules of interaction.

Let users know how to use the stack

Don't lecture your stack's users. Talk to them, invite them to do things, and then invite them to do still more. A stack is more a dialog than a monologue. Break up your text, so users must take action in order to read all of it.

When users make mistakes, provide thoughtful, helpful feedback

Don't be terse or uncommunicative. Tell the user what the error was and what to try instead, if you can. This is especially important in the help section of your stack, where you may be asking your users to try different actions and checking to see if they did them correctly.

The screen on the left in Figure 6-4 provides feedback about the user's error, but no further information. The screen on the right, in contrast, describes the Help button and shows which button it is on screen, before asking the user to try again. This kind of feedback increases the chances that the user's next attempt will be successful.

■ **Figure 6-4**   The screen on the right provides helpful feedback

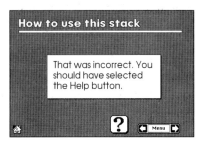

The right tone

The tone of your textual voice is as important as the tone of your visual design. Consideration of your stack's audience, subject matter and presentation helps you decide the correct tone for your stack.

Use humor carefully

Humor can be wonderful to liven up a stack, or it can be deadly. One of the best ways to make sure your humor isn't inappropriate is to keep it out of the way. Use it in examples, not in your directions or interaction with users. Use it in drawings, not in buttons the users must understand and use. Humor should be something the user has the option of noticing, but is not forced to wade through. Remember also that one person's joke can be another's insult. Get feedback from reviewers about the appropriateness of humor.

Praise appropriately when teaching

In the help section of your stack or in training stacks, treat your users with dignity. If you've asked them to do some simple motion, such as clicking a button, respond with a simple "Right" or "Good." Don't say, "Wonderful!!" Avoid exclamation points. Overdone praise can seem insincere or silly.

Be unobtrusive

Users want to use your stack, not accommodate to your personality. The cleaner and more straightforward your text is, the stronger your stack will seem. Develop your voice. See how few words you can use to convey the message. Check that your style of writing doesn't take interest away from the stack's subject matter.

The importance of corrections

Make sure you have the text in your stack reviewed for both content correctness and editorial correctness.

Get subject matter reviews

Regardless of whether you are an expert yourself in the subject matter of your stack, have at least one person who is an expert review the text (and any supporting illustrations) for correct content. Content verification is especially important if the subject of your stack could have potential life-or-death impact, such as a medical information stack or a parts list for aircraft assembly. You would probably want to do intensive content reviews for such subjects. In any case, you don't gain by releasing a stack containing misinformation. Make every effort to provide accurate material. If your information is as good as can be obtained to date, be sure to tell users that up front.

Get editorial help

When users encounter frequent errors in text, they infer that the stack has been sloppily made and may lose confidence in it. Imagine, for example, how teachers would receive your educational stack if it contained any usage, grammar, or spelling errors. Or, as another illustration, you might have an elegant design, beautiful graphics, easy navigation, and incredible scripting, but your users' impression of your stack will be permanently damaged if the title screen says (in New York 24 bold) "Welcom to This Stack."

Even if you are a highly skilled writer yourself, a professional editor or another writer as reviewer can help make sure that your text is polished and error-free. Most important, be sure to have someone other than the writer (and preferably a trained copyeditor or proofreader) go though all the text in the stack one last time after you have made your absolutely final content corrections and before you send the stack off to be mass-produced and distributed.

Fields

If you've decided to use fields for your text, you can choose from several types of fields. (See the "Typography" section of Chapter 4 for information on font selection, line width, and the use of Paint text rather than field text.)

The standard field, available by choosing New Field, can be set to several options: transparent, opaque, or scrolling. You can have several fields on a card, and they can overlap each other.

Transparent fields

Transparent fields are widely used. They're best when you want to present information to the user and make it look as if the information is simply printed on the card, as if it were a piece of paper. Transparent fields are also useful over background graphics.

The example in Figure 6-5 shows the mid-air effect of a transparent field. It gives a freer feeling than text continually bounded by visible boxes. However, as you'll see by comparing Figure 6-5 to the next few examples, it also requires careful screen planning, so that the black text letters don't vanish into the black picture.

■ **Figure 6-5**   An example of a transparent field

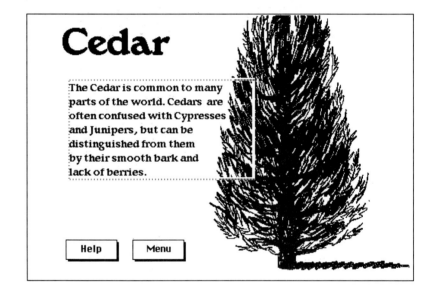

Opaque fields

Opaque fields, when empty, are useful for covering up background text fields, or for blocking out parts of the card while you work on the remainder. Opaque fields have no borders. Other fields that do have borders, such as the rectangle field shown in Figure 6-6, are also opaque. They're also useful when you want the text to sit easily and naturally on top of the graphic, and you want to be able to move the text around, independent of the graphic.

The opaque field shown in Figure 6-6 illustrates the different effect of text sitting directly over a picture. The visual impact of this card is more controlled than that of the previous figure because every element except the illustration of the tree and title is bounded by a black border.

■ **Figure 6-6**   An example of a rectangle field that's opaque

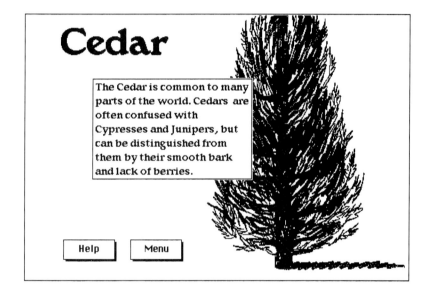

Scrolling fields

Scrolling fields are a mixed blessing. On the one hand, they're a cheap way to put lots of text at the user's disposal, without using much screen space. On the other hand, it's hard to read lengthy text in a scrolling field, and the technique abruptly stops using the visual and audio power of HyperCard, using it only as a text-display tool. Use scrolling fields, but only if you can't come up with a better alternative.

Figure 6-7 shows the same card that you've seen in the past two examples. The scroll bar takes up room in the field, so you can see that the full text no longer fits in the same space, but has scrolled off the bottom. Compare this figure to the previous two, and you'll see that the scroll bar itself makes the screen busier.

■ **Figure 6-7**   An example of a scrolling field

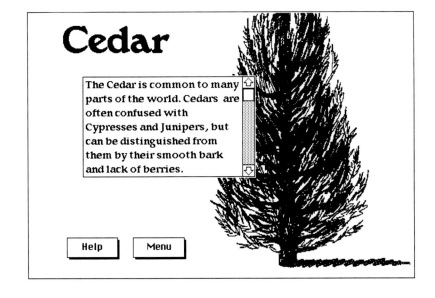

Pop-up fields

A pop-up field is one that appears only as the result of some user action (such as clicking a button) and disappears again when the user clicks in the field or clicks a button to dismiss it. Because pop-up fields are simply text fields that aren't always visible, they can't contain graphics (although you could create the illusion of graphics by making another card that had what appeared to be popped-up text and graphics on it). You can create a button that appears in the pop-up field, but you must explicitly show and hide the button along with the field.

In Figure 6-8, the text field appears in response to the user's clicking on the picture of the cedar tree. Unlike the previous three screens, this one when first opened showed only the word "Cedar," the picture of the tree, and the buttons.

■ **Figure 6-8**   An example of a pop-up field

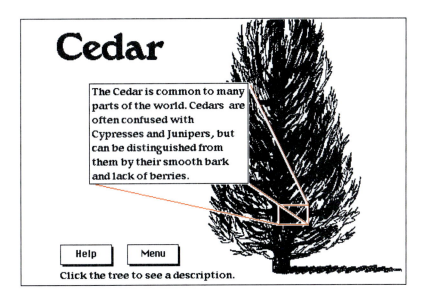

Use pop-up fields for supplementary or "by-the-way" information. Don't use them for critical information, because users may not ever show them. There isn't a standard icon or marker to indicate that a pop-up field even exists on your card; if you decide to use them, standardize their use, teach your users about it in the introduction, and put a reminder of their existence on all cards.

Don't plan to have lots of pop-up fields in one card; they pile up and are hard to read and to close. In general, think hard about having pop-up fields at all; they are extra work for you to make the user aware of their existence, and extra work for the user to make disappear.

Generally, pop-up fields should go away at the user's first click, rather than requiring the user to click an OK button each time. The user may forget to click and continue to the next card; the stack should smoothly put away the fields itself, rather than stopping the user mid-exit.

The following message handler is one suggested technique for doing pop-up fields:

```
on mouseUp
   lock screen --Allows use of visual effect with unlock.
   show card field "pop"
   unlock screen with iris open --Here's the visual effect.
   wait until the mouseClick
   lock screen
   hide card field "pop"
   hide card btn "ok"
   unlock screen with iris close --The reverse effect.
   click at the clickLoc
end mouseUp
```

The first time the handler locks the screen, it puts the pop-up field in place with `show card field "pop"`. Then, with a flourish, it unlocks the screen while doing an iris open visual effect. (You can use visual effect names with the `unlock` command in HyperCard version 1.2 and above only.)

The handler tells HyperCard to wait until the user clicks, and then performs the same action in reverse. Finally, the handler courteously places the pointer at the location where the user clicked (`clickLoc`).

Summary

When writing text for your stack, you have several considerations: accuracy, clarity, and conciseness; readability and flow; grammatical and usage correctness; and appearance on the screen.

Words that are understandable on isolated cards and that flow well across a sequence of cards free the user to focus on the stack's message. Correct grammar, punctuation, and spelling give the user confidence in the stack's accuracy.

Use other people to help prepare the text. Editors, proofreaders, and other writers can catch presentation errors. Subject matter experts can contribute to the stack's breadth, depth, and accuracy. And reviewers or pilot subjects can tell you what the tone sounds like and whether your written instructions are clear.

Music and Sound

SOUNDS AND MUSIC, WHEN USED APPROPRIATELY, CAN AUGMENT YOUR STACK and add a full, rich dimension to the users' otherwise silent experience. Adding sounds to stacks can be as powerful a difference as adding sounds to motion pictures. Consider the effectiveness of the silent movies of the past, when compared to current movies with full soundtracks. The biggest limitation with using sound, today, is the large amount of disk and memory space it requires.

Users' experience with television has accustomed them to sophisticated sound effects just as it has to visual effects. Design your sound to fit the tone of the stack. An amateurish sound effect will give your entire stack an amateurish feel, no matter how rich the graphics. Concentrate on providing sound that's effective and that supports and strengthens the stack's purpose.

Think about whether your stack will be used in a room in which lots of other people are working. Music is generally acceptable if it's not too loud. If you know it will be played repeatedly, make the sound light and avoid a heavy beat.

Always give users the option of turning the sound off completely. Let them know how to turn the sound down on their Control Panel. (If your stack has hidden the menu bar, offer it back to them for a limited time in order to access the Control Panel in the Apple menu.)

Don't make sound the sole conveyer of information. For users who must turn the sound off or who are hearing-impaired, vital information should be conveyed visually as well.

Using short sounds periodically is often more effective than using long sounds or a soundtrack throughout. If you do not have enough disk or memory space to provide continuous sound, try providing short sounds at appropriate places.

Purposes of sound

Sound can be used for many purposes. Understanding the different purposes can help you decide where and when to use sound in your stacks, and whether sound would strengthen your message.

To provide a transition, like a visual effect

One of the most common uses of sound is to reinforce the user's sense of transition. As with visual effects, if you're using sounds this way, be consistent, be brief, and be unobtrusive. Always use the same sound and same visual effect, for instance, to return to the stack's topic list or main menu.

People will associate what they hear with what they see. If one sound is associated with a specific button or icon, people will learn that button's use faster. If selecting the same button produces different sounds in different places, users may become confused.

As with visual effects, the length of the sound conveys information about the importance or kind of transition. A good guide is to have the sound for the transition last roughly the same as the visual effect for the same transition, though sound often begins earlier. The fastest transition for a user, one with no visual effect and no sound, is appropriate for traveling within a section of similar cards. When moving between sections or stacks, however, sounds and visual effects can reinforce the user's sense of location and travel.

The sound in Figure 7-1 begins during the main menu screen on the left, after the user selects the item "Defense." As the card showing the first defense player appears, the sound provides a rippling chord as the transition. The sound fades out after the transition has been made.

■ **Figure 7-1** Sound used to provide a transition from screen to screen

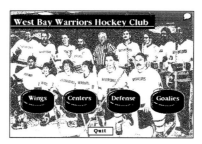
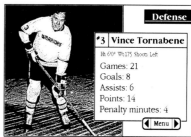

To demonstrate content, like an illustration

Sound is sometimes the point of the stack. Like an illustration, it demonstrates the quality or property that the stack's text discusses. A stack that acts as a catalog for musical instruments, for instance, might let the user hear what the different instruments sound like. A stack for diagnosing disk drive malfunctions might provide sounds of five disk drives with common problems, to help a technician identify a problem. A stack identifying birds might provide both the bird's picture and its song, for users' reference.

When sound is used to demonstrate a point, it should be of excellent quality and should be tested on all possible machine configurations. Alert your users when they open the stack that they should turn up their sound, if it's off. If, as is often the case, the sounds will run more smoothly after the stack is installed on a hard disk, advise your users as soon as the stack opens and before the music begins. If you distribute written documentation for your stack, mention it there as well.

In the example in Figure 7-2, sound informs the user about the stack's content. When the user clicks the "Click to hear sound" button, the sound of the shimmering harp arpeggio is heard. In this example, the sound is a functional part of the stack; like the illustration, it contributes to the content, not to the navigation or overall effect.

■ **Figure 7-2**   Sound that provides content information in a stack

To inform users of progress, like a cursor shape

Sound or music can be a way to tell users that something is happening, even though nothing is visibly changing on the screen. Like the watch cursor, which slowly moves its hands around to indicate progress, sounds can slowly move up in pitch, in speed, or both.

Sounds used for this purpose should be tested for unobtrusiveness, because the user has nothing to do but listen to the sound and may need to hear it repeatedly. Sounds like this are especially good when a long script is running, and the user has little or no visual indication of progress.

Consider using nature sounds, such as water rising in a container, waves coming to shore, or wind rising and fading. Random sounds such as wind through trees or shell windchimes are also an option.

See if there's a sound associated with your application that can give the message. For example, a spreadsheet might use the sound of an adding machine to connote its calculations.

In addition to advising users to adjust the sound level in the Control Panel, you might also consider putting a button in the stack itself, for users' convenience, that toggles the stack's sound on and off.

To give users feedback, like a highlighted button

Sound can give users specific feedback, like an "Auto hilite" button, a dialog box, or a pop-up field. The message can be subtle, such as associating a particular chime with unsuccessful actions, for instance, or direct, such as a voice that tells the user the information.

Sound can give feedback about events that did or did not occur, such as a search that was successfully or unsuccessfully completed (different sounds), a topic that is not covered by the stack, or an illegal user action. Sound can also call the user's attention, such as when used with an "Answer-with" box.

Your specific stack may call for a specific kind of feedback. Consider your stack's purpose and audience when searching for appropriate sounds.

Like illustration and graphics design, sound is culturally dependent. The musical runs illustrated here would sound meaningful to Americans, but not to people from many other cultures. Even the tonal structure built into HyperTalk's `play` command assumes a Western well-tempered scale.

In Figure 7-3, the user is asked what tool the illustration portrays. If, as in the screen on the left, the user clicks the wrong answer, the stack plays a quick series of notes that drops sadly and doesn't resolve. If the user clicks the right answer, the stack provides positive feedback by playing a quick, happy, upward run of notes.

■ **Figure 7-3**   Sound that provides different feedback for wrong and right answers

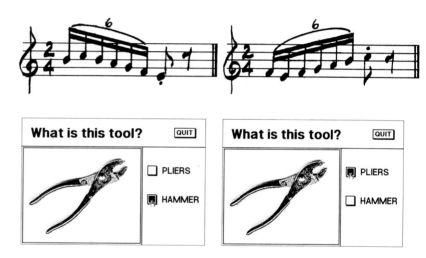

To substitute for animation or graphic information

Sound is sometimes used to substitute for animation or graphic information, especially in providing transitions. If you're watching a movie scene that takes place in an office, and the next scene takes place in the main character's home, the soundtrack might begin playing sounds of the home, such as kids yelling or stereo playing, while the camera is still on the office. After a second or two, the camera simply cuts to the home, without needing to show the character leaving work, driving home, or entering the house. All that graphic information has been replaced by two seconds of sound.

This tradeoff is especially useful when disk space is scarce. Sound and graphics are the two biggest consumers of disk space, and you may find yourself in the position of needing to cut some graphics or sounds. Using sound as a substitute for animation can sometimes save space without sacrificing information.

In Figure 7-4, the two screens illustrate a use of sound as a substitute for animation. In the left, opening screen of the detective game, the user hears footsteps begin. After a few steps, the screen switches to a close-up of the agency's door, and the user knows that he or she is standing outside the door, having walked up to it.

- **Figure 7-4**   Sound that substitutes footsteps for animation to show the transition

To provide a continuous environment, like a movie soundtrack

Some stacks, such as product demonstrations or presentation stacks, are most effective with a continuous soundtrack, like a movie would use. These stacks typically run on hard disks only, because they require several megabytes of memory for the sound alone.

Because space is such a big consideration and potential limiter for these stacks, it's a good idea to hire a professional electronic sound composer, someone who's familiar with computers, with sound equipment, and who can figure out technical ways to put the most sound in the least disk space.

You might consider using pattern music or other cyclic compositions, so that the users hear one long, lovely, rolling sound, even though it's actually one or more shorter sequences, played repeatedly and dovetailed into one another.

As with movies, the sound in stacks should be excellent. Listen to television and movie soundtracks to gather information about what different sound effects convey. Try watching your stack with the sound off, too, to make sure that the graphics and visual effects still convey the essential message.

The sound in Figure 7-5, below, runs as a jazzy, swingy soundtrack accompaniment to a slide-show stack called "World Currency." In this example, sound is not used for isolated effects, transitions, or information, but instead provides a full backdrop and establishes the tone for the stack.

■ **Figure 7-5** Sound that provides a continuous soundtrack throughout stack

Composing sound

Sound, like visual images or written words, can be legally copyrighted and owned by individuals. If you want to use sounds in your stack that were composed by someone else, talk to a lawyer about how to do so. The best way to avoid legal complications is to compose—or have someone compose for you—all the sound for your stack. If you plan to distribute the stack, check with a lawyer about how to establish your ownership of the stack's sounds.

You may have to choose whether to use the available memory space for rich graphics or rich sound. Don't consider attempting full soundtracks without large amounts of space available for your stack.

Computers and sound

Computers store sound differently than tape recorders do. It's not currently possibly to plug a tape recorder into a computer and transfer the sound directly. Instead, you must use special instruments, software, or both to store sounds in a format that both computers and specially built electronic instruments can comprehend. That format is called **MIDI—Musical Instrument Digital Interface.** But after computers have stored sounds, they can, unlike tape recorders, be used to manipulate the sound as if it were any other computer information.

If you begin to work with sound, you will hear about these two kinds of computer (and MIDI) software:

- **samplers,** which act like tape recorders. Samplers record, in MIDI format, any sound they hear. Sampled music is easy to capture and sounds excellent, but uses enormous amounts of disk space.

- **sequencers,** which act like programs. Sequencers take stored sounds and manipulate them. Sequenced music takes more time and skill to compose, but uses far less disk space. The `play` command of HyperCard acts like a sequencer. (The example in the next section shows two short samples, one sounding like a harpsichord and one sounding like a boing).

Five minutes of music can use as little as 62 kilobytes of disk space, using a sequencer, or as much as 6.6 megabytes. Music sounds best if recorded using a sampling rate of 22 kilohertz or higher. Speech, on the other hand, can be recorded at far lower rates and still sound acceptable. Because of this, in a given amount of space you can usually store either a little music or a lot of speech.

As MIDI has caught on and grown in popularity among musicians, companies have begun producing a variety of MIDI instruments—which have the tones inside them—and MIDI controllers, which look like instruments, but actually only control the tones contained in a separate box. In the margin, you can see four kinds of MIDI instruments: a MIDI keyboard, MIDI guitar, MIDI wind controller, and MIDI drum pad controller.

The **MIDI keyboard** is probably the most familiar, since it emulates a piano keyboard and has been the classic input device for electronic music since its inception. Some MIDI keyboards have built-in disk drives for which users can buy a library of disks, the same size as those used by the Macintosh, each with four or five instrument sounds on it. Instead of being limited to the keyboard's sounds, users can simply buy the floppies with the desired instruments.

Keyboard

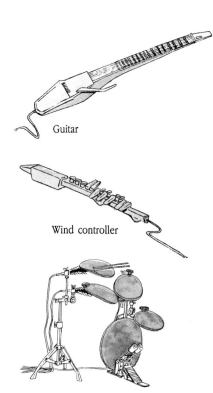

Guitar

Wind controller

Drum pad controller

The **MIDI guitar** was the first non-keyboard MIDI instrument developed. Before its inception, guitarists were barred from the world of MIDI, unless they were willing to learn to play keyboards. With a MIDI guitar, the guitarist simply plays as usual and the sounds are stored directly in the computer.

The **MIDI wind controller** gives MIDI music a vital element: breath. It's fingered like a saxophone, with a similar mouthpiece. If you were to play a breathy note on it, it would send the signal to a MIDI tone generator box. You could then set that tone box to generate the sound of cymbals, and your note would now sound like cymbals. Just as scanners reintroduce the liveliness of hand-drawing to stacks, the MIDI wind controller brings back the liveliness of breath control.

The **MIDI drum pad controller** is set up and played like an ordinary trap set. The musician uses regular drum sticks and foot pedals, and doesn't have to learn any new instrument skills. Instead of tediously entering complex rhythms in the computer, the drummer can simply play the rhythms and let the computer capture the sounds.

How to get sounds into stacks

The easiest way to add sound effects is to use one of the commercially available sound recorders. Some of them come with a microphone and accept both microphone and direct line-in connections from your tape recorder. The best products are those that are designed for HyperCard and produce sound resource files automatically for you. Prepare the sounds or music you want on a tape recorder, then either connect the tape recorder directly, for highest quality, or play the tape into the microphone. The commercial sound recorder will capture the sounds for HyperCard and, ideally, produce sound resources for you to use.

Another way to produce sounds that uses very little disk space is to use HyperCard's play command to write melodies. The play command will play either the standard HyperCard sounds of boing and harpsichord or other sounds you've recorded, at whatever pitch you specify.

To play the familiar melody shown in Figure 7-6, try the handler listed below it in a button script. You'll hear four beeps (one of the standard HyperCard sounds), followed by the melody played on the two standard HyperCard instruments, harpsichord and boing.

■ **Figure 7-6** The children's melody of "Mary had a little lamb" is played twice by the script below

```
on mouseUp
  beep 4
  play "harpsichord" tempo 200 "a4q g f g a a a"
  play "boing" tempo 200 "a4q g f g a a a"
end mouseUp
```

You can also produce your own sound resources. If you had one called MySound for instance, you could use the play command to play it by writing this handler:

```
on mouseUp
  play "MySound" tempo 200 "a4q g f g a a a"
end mouseUp
```

You can vary the tempo and pitch by changing their values in the script. For instance, tempo 100 would be half the speed of tempo 200, and a5 would be an octave higher than a4.

Many sound resources are available as shareware or freeware from users groups. The card shown in Figure 7-7 shows a collection of sound resources, kept as simple play handlers in button scripts. When the user clicks the Applause button, for instance, the sound is heard of thundering applause that quickly dies away. The variety of sounds shown on this card illustrate the range and kinds of sounds stack designers often employ.

■ **Figure 7-7** A card showing collected sound resources, playable by clicking

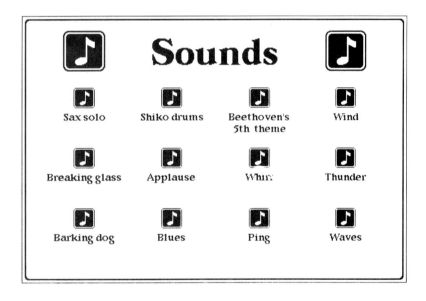

Testing sound

If you are building a stack that will run on several different machines, test your sound early. Because sound takes so much memory and disk space, it may run differently on different machines, or on the same machine with different amounts of memory. A flawless soundtrack on a Macintosh II may stop and start awkwardly on a Macintosh Plus as the Plus hits the limits of memory. As another example, if you're developing on a Macintosh II with 5 megabytes of memory, test your stack on a Macintosh II with 1 megabyte.

Stay in the room during the tests. Notice your own reactions to the sounds. Are there certain sounds that you enjoy every time you hear them? Are there others that become annoying with repetition? Be sure to ask about the stack's sounds in your testing. If people will be using the stack repeatedly, make sure the sound is either pleasant and unobtrusive or under users' control to turn on and off.

Sound is a rich and fertile element to add to HyperCard stacks. If you're just beginning to explore sound, have fun! You might begin by adding only a few sounds to your stacks and using them either at major navigational transition points for emphasis or to alert the user to feedback displayed on the screen. As you continue to use sound, you will probably develop your own style and sense of taste and will begin to accumulate a library of sounds, just as you would a library of designs, graphic images, and visual effects.

Summary

Sound can perform a variety of functions within a stack: provide transitions, illustrate content, convey progress, give feedback, substitute for animation, or provide a continuous environment for the stack. Like graphics and visual effects, sound gives you a vehicle for conveying your message in ways that augment the stack's text.

At its best, sound can enrich and enliven a stack. To keep the user's experience of your stack enjoyable, however, you must place the sound under user control: alert the user to adjust the volume in the Control Panel, and consider providing a button in the stack that turns sound on and off.

Sound is a powerful tone-setter for a stack. When the style of your graphics, writing, and sound all match, users get an integrated, clear message of your stack's purpose. To judge the effectiveness of your stack's sounds, ask other people for their opinions as you develop the stack. Test sound thoroughly, both to make sure that it plays correctly and that it is acceptable to users.

Building Stacks

H OW EXACTLY DOES SOMEONE GO FROM AN IDEA TO A COMPLETED HyperCard stack? The full answer, which would include all the HyperTalk scripting considerations, is beyond the scope of this book. But if you are a beginning stack developer, you may find it useful to study the example of a standard stack-design process, which follows.

If you will be working with a group to design and build a stack, you will find some useful guidelines in the discussion of collaborative stack building later in this chapter.

An example of a standard process

The design process described in this chapter is fairly standard for any product or software development, and includes these steps:

- research
- design and prototype
- development
- production
- testing
- final disk and organizing records
- duplication and distribution

If you've never built a stack before, you might begin by following this model and then adjusting it to suit your personal style. No matter what process you use, the general framework will be similar to the one shown here.

Two characteristics of this process are somewhat different from classical software development, and they are essential for designing useful stacks: Prototyping and iterative development. **Prototyping** means building a bare-bones stack, with card indications such as "Picture of pianist Sarah Walthrop here" and "Text describing her concert schedule and albums here." Prototyping forces you to clarify your design and lets other people review the stack when it's in its most easily changeable state.

The second characteristic, **iterative development,** means that the development phase doesn't consist of building a stack only once. Instead, it means building a version of the stack, getting reviews, deciding on changes, and then repeating this cycle several times. These frequent reviews give you ongoing corrective feedback. Because you don't wait a long time between reviews, you won't be able to veer too far off track.

Two common pitfalls for beginning stack designers are

- doing insufficient research, and then finding out only after weeks of work that (1) your audience is different from what you'd expected, (2) your stack's fundamental design fails to meet your audience's needs, or (3) both

- asking for reviews too late and too infrequently to give you the necessary corrective feedback (the "waiting until it's perfect" syndrome)

Figure 8-1 shows the steps of a standard stack-design process. This chapter and the Stack Design Checklist in Appendix B provide additional detail.

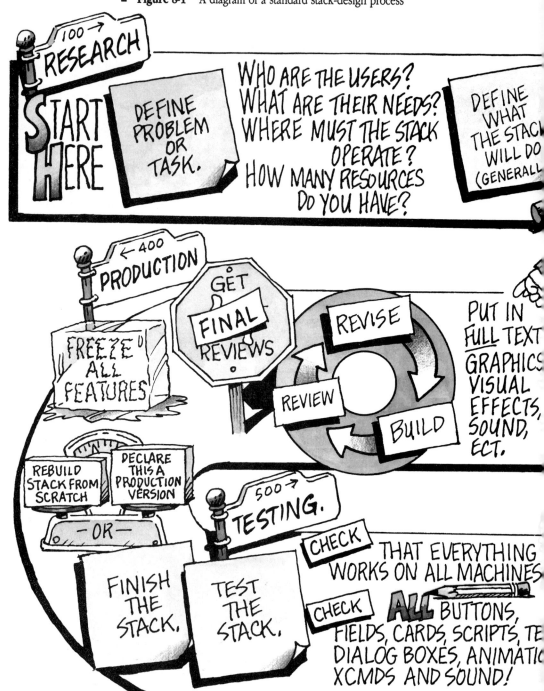

An example of a standard process

Research

The purpose of research is for you to determine the scope of the project and to become educated about it. No question is too simple or obvious to ask; by asking questions, instead of making assumptions, you give your stack development a solid foundation.

Research consists of asking basic questions: Why is this stack needed? What problem is it supposed to solve? Who are the users? With what other equipment or software must this stack work? The answers to these and other questions listed below enable you to write a plan which can be reviewed by others.

Define the problem the stack solves

Defining a problem means describing an undesirable state that exists, not the solution to it. For instance, "People around the company need on-screen graphics and must continually reinvent their own," is a problem statement; "We need an on-line-graphics stack" is not one, since it doesn't allow for multiple solutions. The problem you define sets a general context for the stack, and for your reviewers. It also lets you decide whether a stack is the most effective solution.

Define the stack's users

Decide who your users are. Think of everything you can to specify and identify your users. Use the Stack Design Checklist in Appendix B to help guide you. An example user definition might be "The art directors and graphic designers in my department are the primary users—this stack will completely meet their needs. People across the company who use screen art are secondary users—this stack will meet their needs if possible."

Research what your users need the stack to do

It's critical here to look at the stack from the user's point of view, not yours as the designer. Figure out what the user needs the stack to do generally, such as "Give me on-line access to all the on-screen graphics in the company," and specifically, such as "Let me see the graphics; let me sort through them by categories; let me print them as well as see them on screen." These user needs are the cornerstones of your design.

Define the environment in which the stack must run

Environment includes the entire surroundings in which the stack will operate: equipment, people, and paper (such as existing workbooks or manuals with whose typefaces or content the stack must be consistent). Environment includes things like the kinds of machines and amounts of memory the stack must run on, the network connections or other machines with which it must interact, if any, and the situation in which the user will interact with the stack. An environment description might say something like "The stack must run on a Macintosh II with 2 megabytes of memory, fit on one 800K disk, access a central database of graphics on some network device, and be usable by several individuals in my department simultaneously."

State your resources and limitations in developing the stack

Describe what you have available to develop the stack: people, skills, money, time, machines, assumptions, risks, context, and relationship to other pertinent items, such as books, courses, or disks. This description lets your reviewers help you determine whether your plan is reasonable. If your plan says you will store 50,000 graphic images for your stack to access, for instance, and you have no one available to put those images into electronic form, this step helps you recognize that need.

Define the general solution: summarize what the stack will do

You began by stating a problem that your stack would solve. Now it's time to summarize the solution, given all the research you've done so far. The example problem above, "People around the company need on-screen graphics and must continually reinvent their own," can now be addressed by the solution, "We'll provide an on-line graphics stack. It will be a stack for people in this department that lets several people simultaneously access a central database of graphics on a network file server. The stack will fit on one 800K disk and give the user the ability to see, sort, and print the images."

Capture all the research in a written plan

Write down your research and plans. This is partially for other people, so that they can help you review your approach most effectively, and partially for you, so that as you dive into design and development, you have a touchstone to return to. Often, during the reviews, people will come up with endless ideas for additional functionality and features. One way to sort out which ones to implement is to return to this written plan and see which ones directly further your goals or the needs of your primary users.

Get reviews on the plan and general approach

Send your written plan out for review. This review can be as formal or as informal as you wish, but it's one of the two most critical review points. (The second is the reviews you get on the prototype.) If you are heading in the wrong direction, or incorrectly analyzing your users' needs, this is the time to find out, not after you've built 450 cards. Include among your reviewers representative users to check that your direction meets their needs, stack builders to check that your approach is realistic, managers or clients to check that the costs, time, and skills are feasible, and some people whose sound judgment and common sense you trust.

Design and prototype

In this stage, you make many decisions about how the stack will look and act, and you build a sketchy prototype version with which to solicit reviews. Often the prototype elicits more useful feedback than the written plan did; by completing a prototype early, therefore, you will get the information you need to begin development with confidence.

The design will change several times during development. But by producing a prototype, you ensure that large changes can be addressed early, freeing subsequent versions to act as refinements to a generally acceptable design.

Look at similar stacks; brainstorm; develop a vision

Look at the networks, the user groups, and any other stack collections you can find. Search for similar stacks to get ideas about how other designers have approached similar problems. You may not find any that are exactly like the stack you're building. You may also discover good interface ideas in completely unrelated stacks. This is a "widening step," to take in fuzzy information about your stack and let ideas roll around in your mind. Develop a vision of what you'd like your stack to look and feel like to the user.

Decide what your stack will do, in more detail

After all the brainstorming and inspiration of the previous step, this is the "narrowing" step, where you decide exactly what your stack needs to do to implement the functionality outlined in your plan. To continue with the graphics example, you might at this point decide that your stack needed to provide a local interface to a remote file server; to display both rough and final images; and to let the user sort by the image's topic, by its illustrator, by its style (hand-drawn line art, photographic, or computer-generated), or by its creation date.

Design your first pass at the stack's visual and user interface

The purpose of this step is to make enough decisions that you can build a skeleton of the stack. This means you don't need to decide details such as typography, but you do need to decide how the stack will work.

Decide how the stack will present its information to the user. Consider underlying metaphor, stack structure, and navigation methods. Think about how the stack will open. Decide what script and XCMD functionality you'll need. Decide roughly how you will use graphics, text, sound, visual effects, and animation to interact with the user.

You may begin by diagramming and sketching on paper, or you may begin directly on screen. You probably won't decide all the details in this step, but you need to decide enough of them to let you begin building your stack.

Build a skeleton of the stack

After you have the design roughed out, it's time to begin working on screen if you haven't already. Card layout, for instance, can be sketched on paper, but is much easier to manipulate on screen. Your task now is to build a skeletal stack that uses your first pass at the interface and does what it's supposed to. Some parts may be missing, and everything is subject to change. The purpose is not to build a beautiful final version, but to build a sketchy one with which to elicit reviews.

You now have your navigation, environment, and stack structure roughed out, either on paper or in your mind. You may have some possibilities done on screen. To build your prototype:

- get a current copy of HyperCard and the Macintosh system software
- check to make sure that none of your software has been infected by a virus. (If you need information on how to do this, contact one of the user groups listed in the Preface.)
- create a new stack
- build an opening card
- build a main menu or stack map card to serve as your guide

- put all-purpose travel buttons (forward, backward, return to menu) in the background

- make destination cards for each item listed on your menu or stack map, giving the different sections different backgrounds, if needed

- type each card's name in a field on it, such as "Graphics display card," or "Help card," so you can tell where you are

- include placeholder cards for your opening screen, introduction, help, and whatever other parts of the stack you've designed

- add button scripts to your main menu or stack map, so that when you click on a topic, you go to the correct destination

This structure may not be completely detailed; for instance, you may have designed an entire section called "Help," but in this skeleton have only a single placeholder card for it. The placeholder at least lets both you and your reviewers get a sense of what you intend for the final stack.

Add indications of text, graphics, sound, visual effects, animation, basic scripts, and XCMDs to the stack skeleton

Go through your skeleton and indicate what will be on each card. The purpose of these indications is to give the reviewers a clear idea of the final intended stack, so that they, in turn, can give you useful feedback.

Your indications may consist of things as basic as "Four buttons here, to let user select graphics by style, illustrator, date, and topic" or as elaborate as the four buttons designed the way you want them to look, which work as intended when the user clicks them.

Whether the functionality and interface elements actually exist or not, include at least descriptions of what you intend. These may also include notes to yourself, such as, "Note—ask John Dimmick if it's possible to animate a brush, painting the title on an easel in opening section."

You now have a prototype of your stack. People looking at it can either experience directly or read on screen its intended function and interface. You may want to begin lining up graphic designers, writers, subject matter experts, and music composers at this point.

Get reviews on the prototype

This is the second most critical review of all the ones you'll get. (The first was on the written design plan.) People may have envisioned something quite different from what you're going to build; it's much better to find out at this stage than after you've begun implementing the stack in full and glorious detail. Get reviews from the same kinds of people that reviewed your plan, but this time pay particular attention to the users.

Do informal user testing. Ask potential users if this would fully meet their needs when implemented, and, if not, what would make the stack more useful and usable. Watch them. Where do they get lost or confused? Listen to them. One quiet comment now may save you weeks of wasted work.

Development

During development, you work toward completion of the project, getting plenty of reviews as you go. Plan on the design changing and evolving during this step in response to your reviewers' comments and to your own growing understanding of the stack. The stack will go from a sketchy skeleton to a near-final version in this step.

Change the design as needed, in light of the prototype reviews

After you've gotten feedback on the prototype, you will probably want to make changes to the design, the interface, the navigation, or the functionality of the stack. You may even need to change the information you had outlined in your original plan, if you've discovered your assumptions about audience, purpose, limitations, or user needs were wrong. By making these changes to the design and to the prototype, you've entered the Development phase.

Build a fleshed-out version of the stack

Begin keeping date-and-time version information for each stack. The best place to keep this information is in the box available through the File menu's Get Info command, in the Finder. Begin keeping copies of the stack, frozen at various points. Begin making backup copies of the current master.

Fill in the details. Finish writing the scripts and XCMDs. Write any remaining text. Put in the visual effects. Work on typography, graphic design, and illustration. Add initial sound, perhaps. Add rough animation, if you call for it.

If you plan to use professional graphic designers or professional composers, now is the time to involve them. Explain to them as clearly as possible what you want. "I want classical music" is not as descriptive as "I want something like Pachelbel's Canon in D."

If your stack provides expert information, as a medical stack might, have a subject matter professional evaluate the stack's accuracy. Have the text and overall fit of the different design elements evaluated and corrected by someone other than yourself (or the writer), preferably by a professional editor.

Get reviews as you finish sections or make big changes

Develop the habit of getting reviews regularly. Choose the points at which you want reviews. Useful points are when you've completed a section, when you've made major changes to the interface, or when you've made changes to address a specific user need that arose out of earlier testing. For instance, if your first round of user testing said that the opening screen was too full and confusing, and you've now divided that information into two screens, you might want to get reviews only on that change.

Be specific about the purpose of the review or the user testing. Say, for example, "I want you to tell me if this section gives you the capability you want. I don't care as much about how it looks, yet, because I haven't worked on that." Don't sabotage your test, though; if you're testing whether the user can navigate successfully, for example, don't explain how all the buttons work and where they take the user.

Often a simple change can make a huge difference in users' perception of the stack. It's still not too late to make fundamental changes to the interface and the design. The most important feedback and design changes, in these early stages, are those that focus on the overall environment, metaphor, navigation, and structure of the stack. These considerations are far more important at this stage than the spelling of a word or shading of an illustration.

Repeat the cycle of build–review–revise several times

Continue building the stack, getting reviews or user test results, and changing the stack according to that feedback. As the review process continues, and your navigation and structure solidify, you increasingly want feedback to change focus to the details of the graphic design, illustrations, typography, wording, grammar, animation, and sound.

Hold your final development review

At some point, your stack is fairly set. It does what you intend, with the interface, navigation, and introduction you intend, and with all the appropriate graphics, text, sounds, and transitions. If you haven't had your stack reviewed by your lawyer, do so at this point. Consciously choose a review date and tell reviewers, "After this one, I'm entering production and finishing the stack. No more developmental changes unless I've really missed the boat. No more added functional capability. This is it, folks, and this is your last chance to give me any suggestions for changes."

Production

During production, the emphasis shifts from building and evolving the stack to finishing the stack. Instead of adding features, concentrate on completing and honing what you have. You may decide to build a clean production version of the stack from scratch, or you may choose a current version and declare it the production version. Either way, your purpose is to now create the finished stack.

Freeze all features

The most salient characteristic of the Production phase is that you stop adding features. Design and development, the change-oriented phases, are done. The focus is now on finishing the stack, making sure every part works, and creating a final, error-free version of the disk.

Option 1: Rebuild the stack cleanly, from scratch

There are two ways that people begin the production phase. The first way is to look at the often-patched current version of the stack and now, knowing exactly what it will contain, rebuild a clean version from scratch, possibly with better or more centralized algorithms or with cleaned-up backgrounds.

Option 2: Declare the latest version to be the production version

The other way developers proceed is to declare the latest version of the stack to be the production version, and simply keep working with it. In this case, it's important to tell yourself and your reviewers that you have entered the production phase.

Finish the stack completely

Finish all those details you've saved for last: the image you've included but aren't sure you have legal permission to use . . . the intermittent but fairly harmless bug you haven't tracked down in one XCMD . . . the place where sound hiccups as it's playing . . . the typo you never corrected. Now is the time to fix every last little glitch.

Check the stack yourself

Go through the stack one last time yourself with a meticulous eye. Look at every detail. Check all the buttons. Fix the bugs and errors you find. Careful as you may be, however, there are always some errors that elude you, simply because you're so familiar with the stack.

Testing (by you and others)

Your final testing should be rigorous and thorough. It's the last chance to find any hidden problems. Testing may be partially done by you, but will be most effective if done by other people. Make sure everything works in the stack. Check the stack on all configurations of memory and machines on which you intend the stack to run.

Make sure everything works

This is a detailed, repetitive, essential step. Have someone else test every button, command, and dialog box option. Check animation for speed and smoothness, for visual impact, and for synchronization with sound. Evaluate visual effects for consistency. Check sound for volume, pace, and smoothness. Edit writing for flow, typographical or grammatical errors, and consistent font usage. Check button, field, and graphic placement on the card. Make sure the correct backgrounds are within the sections. Verify scripts' and XCMDs' functionality: do they do what they're supposed to, with no side effects? Confirm that names on the sections match the names on the menus.

Make sure cards are in logical order, so users who give a `show all cards` command get a coherent picture of the stack. Putting cards in logical order is important because many experienced stack users have seen so many stacks with poor navigation that they use the `show all cards` command automatically to make sure they see everything. Although you don't need to put cards in logical order for the stack to function, doing so is a mark of clarity, courtesy, and professionalism.

Try to break the stack

Have someone else deliberately try to break the stack, and offer rewards for every successful destruction. Deliberately do the opposite of what's asked. Type ahead (or click buttons ahead) rapidly, and see what happens. Consider using junior high or high school students to help. Seek people who are unfamiliar with HyperCard.

Check the stack on all machines and memory configurations

Check the stack on all the machines and memory configurations on which you intend the stack to run. Sound-intensive and graphics-intensive stacks, especially, run differently on the Macintosh Plus than on the Macintosh II, and differently with 1 megabyte of memory than with 8 megabytes. You may want to keep two machines continually running as you design and develop the stack, one with the minimum memory and power, the other with the maximum, to check on your stack's performance.

Check for viruses on your master disk

An essential, citizenly step before declaring your disk final is to check it for all known viruses. Nothing will kill your stack faster than a reputation as a virus spreader. If you don't know how to detect a virus, contact your local user group to learn (see the Preface for details).

Final disk

This is the moment you've been building towards: The stack does what it's supposed to, without error, and with elegance and grace. You have a final disk to use for duplication and distribution.

Organize and celebrate

Because most stacks need to be revised at some point, either by their original designer (you) or by some other designer, it is essential that while the entire project is fresh in your memory you organize all disks, scripts, XCMDs, files, graphics, sounds, reports, and written documents relating to this stack.

Have a big party! You have successfully designed and completed your stack.

Duplication, distribution, and maintenance

Duplication and distribution, the steps where you make as many copies of your stack as necessary and send them into the world to your users, are beyond the scope of this book to discuss. However, they are the next steps in the product development process, followed by maintenance, which often includes revisions and upgrades to the stack. During maintenance you'll be profoundly grateful to yourself for organizing your records. Maintenance continues for as long as you care to support and distribute the stack.

Collaborative stack building

Collaborative stack building is a relatively common method of developing applications and utilities in HyperCard, because so many diverse skills are necessary to design a first-rate stack. This shared development process has advantages and disadvantages; some people love it, some people hate it. Sometimes a subject matter expert and a stack designer collaborate. Other times an entire team works together to design and build a stack. Collaboration differs from single-author development in some important ways.

Group collaboration has the following advantages:

- More skills are available to do the work.

- Two or more parts of a stack can be developed simultaneously.

But collaboration can also have the following costs:

- All participants' roles must be explicitly clarified, and an ongoing process set for discussing how roles shift and change.

- Frequent and efficient communication is needed among the stack-building team, including a strategy for tracking and updating the most recent, "master" copy of the stack.

The skills needed to design a stack include instructional design, user interface design, graphic design, writing, scripting, XCMD programming, and music composition. When these skills are distributed among several people (scripter plus illustrator plus writer, for instance, or designer plus scripter), the stack has the potential of being richer than any one person could make it.

Yet the time saved by helping hands can also be time lost if communication among the team members is not accurate and efficient.

Some techniques exist for helping to make collaboration an efficient and enjoyable experience. If you are part of such a team, your group should determine three essential things before work begins: roles and responsibilities, ground rules, and communication methods.

Roles and responsibilities

Who does what? Because the skills of instructional design, user interface design, writing, graphic design, scripting, and music composition can fall differently in different combinations of people, it's important to define who's going to do each of these tasks.

Although two-person or even three-person teams may work well in an equal collaboration, large teams will work far more smoothly and efficiently when one person has the final decision-making authority on the stack's content.

The roles that your team will need to assign, even if it's only a team of two people, include

- instructional designer
- user interface designer
- writer
- graphic designer
- sound composer
- HyperTalk scripter
- XCMD programmer (if needed; may be same person as scripter, may not)
- final decision authority for schedule, content, and resources
- tester, editor, and other key reviewers who are also project participants
- clerical and logistical support

Sometimes assigning these roles is easy, especially when one person on the team is hiring others. Even in this case, however, it's best to review assumptions about roles before proceeding.

Ground rules

The secret to good communication is having ground rules. These are agreements about how to communicate. Adhering to ground rules can prevent many of the common communication problems that arise, especially if you make them the rules early and revisit them periodically.

Establish your ground rules early, and write them down. Among the ground rules you may want to establish are the agreements you make about

- who does what
- who has the final say
- how often, when, and where you meet
- how you record team agreements (on paper? on disk? on a flip chart?)
- what the goal is, and how team members will know if it changes
- how you track the master stack on disk
- how the team can change the ground rules

Ground rules are not necessarily democratic, but they must address the needs of all team members.

If you begin your collaboration by discussing ground rules, you'll have provided a good basis for team communication.

Communication methods

Keep it simple and use what works. Every team is different, so find the simplest method of communication that satisfies all your team members' needs.

Paper   One common communication method is to use paper. Provide a written design plan, listing the stack's audience, subject matter, presentation, and resource limitations; draw a stack map, laying out how the stack will work; write and sketch a script or storyboard, showing how text and illustrations align; and write up meeting notes, schedules, or summaries of group agreements or plans.

Team headquarters   Another common method is to designate one place as team headquarters, and keep on the wall a bulletin board full of note cards pinned up to represent the stack. This area will become a natural meeting place, since people can refer to the stack pinup, and, when all are present, change it on the spot without needing any further communication. Some teams use an electronic team headquarters, by using a network file server to store all versions of the stack and all team communications.

Project style reference   Groups make agreements about ground rules, about how to proceed, and about style conventions. It's important to make a style sheet or on-line repository for this stack's conventions of, among other things, graphic look, button kind and design, fonts, card layout, illustrations, spelling, text, navigation, and user interface.

Master copy of the stack

One of the biggest concerns of collaborative stack-building is keeping track of the version that has the latest changes, known as the "master," and ensuring that changes are being made to the master and not, inadvertently, to old copies.

Keep track of stacks by versions. Don't use only a version number, such as "Version 1"; instead, use a title that includes date, time, and author, such as "6/15/89 3:45 p.m. - Version 1.0 - JHerman" or "890615 09:45 - Version 1.0 - JHerman." Keep this information in the box available by selecting the File menu's Get Info command from the Finder. It's important to keep your notes here because the stack's version date as recorded by the Finder will get updated every time the stack is opened, even if nothing has been changed. This careful tracking may seem like overkill in the beginning, but it can save hours or days of reconstruction in the end.

There are a couple different methods to keep track of the master (and you may have your own, as well). One way is to designate a "master keeper," one person who makes all the changes to the master; everyone else indicates changes on paper. Another way is to "pass the baton"—make a single (frequently backed up) disk, mark it with a special pen or color so it stands out, and pass it to whoever needs it next. If you have a large team, you might even keep a chart in some visible place that says who has the master checked out. This system will cut down on the extraneous communication time.

To keep track of what the master currently includes and which changes to it have not yet been made, consider making a printed book of all the screens. Reviewers and team members can indicate needed changes by adding notes on stick-on tags to the book (or by inserting colored blank pages with comments), which you then can check off as you make the changes. This will give you a visual indication of how many planned changes you have remaining.

Regular meetings

Setting a regular team meeting time is a good way to minimize time otherwise spent in communication. When team members know they can count on a regular, probably weekly, meeting, they'll save their issues and concerns for the meeting instead of contacting their teammates individually.

The agenda for a team meeting is best set at the beginning of the meeting. Ask team members what items they want on the agenda, write those down, and then cover those during the meeting. Knowing that everyone's concerns will be addressed makes team members see these meetings as their own, and thus as valuable and contributory.

Summary

Designing stacks is a matter of following a fairly standard process. By beginning with research and a written plan, then building a sketchy prototype, you'll elicit the reviews you need to give your stack a firm foundation. Continue to change and evolve the stack during development, then freeze all features as you begin producing the final stack. Test the stack rigorously; after testing you will have a final disk—celebrate! Then organize your records, files, and scripts. Duplicate and distribute the stack, and the only thing remaining is to support the stack.

Because so many skills are needed to build a stack—instructional design, user interface design, graphic design, writing, sound composition, HyperTalk scripting, and XCMD programming—you may decide to collaborate with other people. If you do collaborate, it's advisable to define people's roles, establish team communication methods, and decide how to track the "master" copy of the stack. These techniques will help enable your team to function smoothly and effectively.

Human Interface Design: Ten General Principles

Users EXPECT EVERY MACINTOSH APPLICATION TO BE USER-CENTERED, SIMPLE, and easy to learn. Your stack is no exception. This chapter briefly outlines the ten general design principles presented in the book *Human Interface Guidelines: The Apple Desktop Interface*, published by Addison-Wesley.

About users

The Human Interface Design Principles are based on some assumptions about people. A good interface allows people to accomplish tasks. Tasks will vary, but people share some common characteristics.

People are instinctively curious; they want to learn, and they learn best by active self-directed exploration of their environment. People strive to master their environment; they like to have a sense of control over what they are doing, to see and understand the results of their own actions. People are skilled at manipulating symbolic representations; they love to communicate in verbal, visual, and gestural languages. Finally, people are most productive and effective when the environment in which they work and play is enjoyable and challenging.

General design principles

This section describes the ten fundamental Human Interface Design Principles and discusses how each applies to designing stacks. Briefly, these principles involve

- use of metaphors
- direct manipulation
- see-and-point (instead of remember-and-type)
- consistency
- WYSIWYG (what you see is what you get)
- user control
- feedback and dialog
- forgiveness
- perceived stability
- aesthetic integrity

Metaphors from the real world

- Use concrete metaphors and make them plain, so that users have a set of expectations to apply to computer environments.

- Whenever appropriate, use audio and visual effects that support the metaphor.

People have more experience with the real world than they do with computers. To take advantage of their experience, use metaphors in your stacks that correspond to the everyday world.

HyperCard is already based on a real-world metaphor, the "card." People are familiar with using cards to organize information. The card metaphor allows users to make some important assumptions about how HyperCard works: users assume that cards can be grouped together into "stacks," that they can have both text and pictures on them, and that they can be changed or updated.

If you decide to use a new metaphor in your stack, think about how the new metaphor will affect users' expectations. For instance, a book metaphor would imply that information is presented in a linear format, that travel is limited to "forward," "backward," and "turn-to-a-given-page," and that it's possible to see all pages by simply going forward until the end.

Before you select a metaphor for your stack, make sure the content of the stack lends itself to the metaphor. Real-world metaphors tend to help users understand how to use a stack, but it's better to have no metaphor at all than to force your content into an inappropriate one.

Direct manipulation

- Users want to feel that they are in charge of the computer's activitites.

- Tell users their options by providing visible choices, ways to make their choices, and feedback acknowledging their choices.

This principle is based on the assumption that people learn best by active, self-directed exploration. People expect their physical actions to have physical results, and they want their tools to provide feedback. This feedback can be provided visually, audibly, or both.

Highlight topics of interest. Show the user what options are available. If an option is normally available, but not in a specific case, convey that information by providing a "grayed-out" version of it. If grave consequences will follow from choosing an option, warn the user before any damage is done. If a particular command is being carried out, provide visual clues. If the command can't be carried out, tell the users why it can't be carried out. Also tell them what they can do instead.

See-and-point (instead of remember-and-type)

- Users select actions from alternatives presented on the screen.

- Users rely on recognition, not recall; they shouldn't have to remember anything the computer already knows.

- Most programmers have no trouble working with interfaces that require memorization. The average user is not a programmer.

Stacks are visually and spatially oriented. The way everything appears—text, graphics, buttons, options—should be consistent and well thought out. Users should be able to anticipate what will happen when they interact with your stack by choosing objects, activities, and options.

Don't force users to remember the possible destinations and ways of getting around your stack; keep those options present on the screen, and make their use clear. Most stacks will have two kinds of see-and-point navigation options on the screen: those that are available at all times, such as Help, Return to Start, or Quit HyperCard, and those that are card specific.

There can be advantages—such as speed—to the "remember-and-type" approach. If you decide to offer keystroke alternatives, offer them in addition to, not in place of, the on-screen methods. Users who are new to your stack or who are looking for potential actions in a confused moment, must always be able to find a desired option on the screen.

Just as the average user is not a programmer, the average user is not a HyperCard power user. Don't rely on the user's knowledge of keyboard shortcuts to navigate. In fact, don't rely on the user's knowledge of stacks or HyperCard at all. Set up an environment, teach the user about it, and provide see-and-point ways to use and navigate through it.

Consistency

Effective applications are both consistent within themselves and consistent with one another.

Consistency within a stack is essential. The look, the usage, and the stack behavior should be the same throughout. The way the user does things should always be consistent within a stack. For example, your stack should have a consistent design for these elements:

- graphic look
- grouping of buttons
- placement of buttons
- visual and audio feedback
- card layout
- background for cards with similar functions
- stack structure

Consistency in these elements makes it easier for the user to focus on the content of the stack.

If you plan to use any of the standard elements of the Apple Desktop Interface in your stack (such as menus, dialog boxes, and so forth) follow the guidelines presented in *Human Interface Guidelines: The Apple Desktop Interface.*

WYSIWYG (what you see is what you get)

- There should be no secrets from the user, no abstract commands that only promise future results.
- There should be no significant difference between what the user sees on the screen and what eventually gets printed.

The WYSIWYG principle has special significance in stack modeling and navigation. The layout of your stack should not, except in special cases, be a secret to your user. Part of "What you see is what you get" is letting the users know what they're seeing, and how it relates to the whole stack.

If you provide a representation of your stack, such as a stack map, table of contents, or menu, that representation should contain an accurate and complete model. Nothing frustrates a user more than finding a part of the stack that's not on the stack map, or discovering that the stack's true structure isn't anything like what the menu implied. Make coherent models and communicate them. Let the users know where they are in relation to the whole. Provide a map, but also provide "You-are-here" indicators, or names for the individual screens.

User control

■ The user, not the computer, initiates and controls all actions.

People learn best when they're actively engaged. Too often, the computer acts and the user merely reacts. Or, the computer "takes care" of the user, offering only those alternatives that are judged "good" for the user or "protect" the user from detailed deliberations.

This protective approach may seem appealing, but it puts the computer, not the user, in the driver role. In most cases, it's better to let the user try risky things. You can provide warnings, but let the action proceed if the user confirms that this action is indeed desired. This approach protects the beginner but allows the user to remain in control.

Get your user doing something quickly. Good stacks are interactive. Many stacks begin with an "attract mode," where the screen is alive with inviting animation, rich graphics, and the words "Click to begin."

Let the user choose what happens next, both in using the stack and in navigating around it. This is especially important when offering long animation or sound sequences.

Suppose you wanted your stack to provide a slide show with accompanying music. A frustrating implementation, giving the user no control, would start the slide show and music the instant the stack opened, and run for several (possibly loud) minutes until done. An implementation that gives the user more control might open on a screen that indicates the length of the slide show, asks the user to set the volume level or turn off sound, provides a button called "Start slide show" and displays an unobtrusive sentence, saying "Click any time to interrupt."

Feedback and dialog

- Keep the user informed.
- Provide immediate feedback.
- Make user activities simple at any moment, though they may be complex taken together.

To be in charge, the user must be informed. When, for example, the user initiates an operation, your stack should provide immediate feedback to confirm that the operation is being carried out, and (eventually) that it's finished.

Immediate feedback can be provided by buttons that become highlighted, click, beep, or display a visual effect. For time-consuming operations, feedback can be provided by temporarily changing the cursor into a watch or beach ball or by displaying a message that explains the reason for the delay.

If an operation can't be completed, tell the user why it can't be completed. This communication should be brief, direct, and expressed in the user's vocabulary, not the stack designer's or the programmer's.

Forgiveness

- Users make mistakes; forgive them.
- The user's actions are generally reversible—let the users know about any that aren't.
- Users get lost in stacks; help them find their way.

Most users don't like to read manuals. They would rather figure out how something works by exploration, with lots of action and lots of feedback.

As a result, users sometimes make mistakes or explore further than they really wanted to. Forgiveness means letting users do anything reasonable, letting them know they won't break anything, always warning them when they're entering risky territory, then allowing them either to back away gracefully or plunge ahead, knowing the consequences.

When options are presented clearly, with appropriate and timely feedback, alert messages should be infrequent. If the user receives a barrage of alert messages, gets lost frequently, or can't figure out how to use the stack, something is wrong with the stack's design.

Perceived stability

- Users feel comfortable in a computer environment that remains understandable and familiar rather than changing randomly.

People use computers because computers are versatile and fast. Computers can calculate, revise, display, and record information far faster than people can. If users are to cope with the complexity a computer handles so easily, they need some stable reference points.

These stable reference points are established by how your stack looks, how it acts, and how it feels. You are setting up an implicit contract with your user about the rules of this particular environment, and those rules should be clear and communicated.

Most important, your stack should provide conceptual stability. Give your user a consistent model for how to perceive the stack's function and structure. Note the emphasis on "perceived"; a user may *perceive* your stack to have a single-frame, tree, or network structure, even though in *fact* all stacks are linear sequences of cards, with different navigational control structures superimposed. Provide a clear, finite set of options, and tell the user what they are.

Your stacks should also provide visual stability. Provide a constant overall look and graphic design for your stack. Design the card layout to be constant for similar cards and visually related for all cards in the stack. Place your buttons in reliable and functionally grouped locations. Use a consistent button design; If you're using the same button on several cards, don't represent the button by an icon on one card and a text label on another.

The illusion of stability is what's important. The environment can and should change as users interact with it, but should give users a number of familiar landmarks to rely upon.

Aesthetic integrity

- Visually confusing or unattractive displays detract from the effectiveness of human–computer interactions.

- Different "things" should look different on the screen.

- Messes are acceptable only if the user makes them—stacks aren't allowed this freedom.

In traditional computer applications, the visual appearance of the screen has been a low priority and consequently somewhat arbitrary. In contrast, HyperCard stacks *depend* upon the visual appearance of the screen. As much as possible, commands, features, parameters, choices, navigational options, and data should appear as graphic objects on the screen.

People deserve and appreciate attractive surroundings. Consistent visual and audible communication is very powerful in delivering complex messages and opportunities simply, subtly, and directly.

Summary

These ten general design principles form a powerful basis for designing and evaluating your stacks. These principles provide general guidance. Most people don't have extensive backgrounds in user interface design; following these ten principles is a simple way to make your stacks more usable. A single principle, such as that of user control, can guide many decisions, from giving users buttons with which to control their navigation to giving them volume controls with which to turn sound up, down, or off.

If you plan to use elements from the standard Macintosh desktop interface, get the book *Human Interface Guidelines: The Apple Desktop Interface,* published by Addison-Wesley. In addition to discussing these design principles, this book specifies in detail how elements such as a Macintosh window, dialog box, or pull-down menu should act.

Special Markets

T HIS APPENDIX CONTAINS AN OVERVIEW OF DESIGN AND SCRIPTING
considerations for international products and for products for people with
disabilities. This appendix provides overall awareness and some useful rules of
thumb in designing for special markets; it is not a detailed specification.

International markets

If you are designing stacks to be used in more than one country, it's most important to decide which countries you're planning to target. "International" is a vague term. "Chinese, French, and Norwegian," for example, is a more specific description.

Either you or people from other countries may want to translate your stacks, and thus "localize" them. Whenever possible the translation should be done by a someone who is both a native speaker of the language and familiar with the scripting conventions of the country. The next best choice is to use a native speaker as a reviewer or editor.

If you know your stack will be shipped to more than one country, there are some simple preventive guidelines to follow as you design and script your stack. Interface design considerations refer to how the stack is perceived by users. Scripting considerations refer to how the stack is perceived by you or other scripters who need to translate the stack's HyperTalk script.

Interface design considerations

Because each country is different, interface design decisions will differ for each culture. In general, be aware that symbols, colors, and sounds are culturally dependent and carry different connotations in different countries.

These are some interface design decisions to keep in mind as you design your stack:

- Allow about 30% more space for text, because many translations take more space than English.
- Use regular text in fields, not Paint text.
- Use culturally neutral or appropriate graphics, symbols, and icons.
- Use culturally neutral or appropriate sounds and music.

Text

Plan extra space into the layout of your text. Fields and buttons on which text appears may need to contain up to 30% more text after the English has been translated.

The English alphabet is, like that of French or German, based on a Roman alphabet. Non-Roman fonts, like Arabic or Japanese, are generally more complex, and therefore need to be larger so users can make out the details. Some non-Roman fonts are unreadable on screen if they're in nine-point type, for instance.

Put your text in text fields, instead of using Paint text. Paint text normally has some advantages, such as allowing you to rotate it and avoiding problems with users who don't have your fonts. But for translating stacks, regular text in fields is better because the translators can quickly find the text and easily translate it, without having to redraw it. There is currently no way to search for Paint text. You'll save disk space, too, by putting text in fields.

Graphics and sound

Choose culturally neutral or appropriate graphics, symbols, and icons, such as the international traffic and road sign icons. If you know exactly which countries you're designing for, you can choose more specific symbols. Make sure they're appropriate for those intended countries.

Another solution is to substitute words for graphics, especially on buttons. Instead of a question mark icon for a "Help" button, for instance, use a named button labeled "Help." Translations from English into other languages often require more room, so as you work on your button design, leave room for longer names.

When choosing symbols and images of people in your stacks, be sure to avoid nationalist imagery. What's patriotic or inspiring in one culture may be incomprehensible or offensive in another.

Sounds and music also carry cultural connotations. Music composed using the `play` command, for instance, is limited to the notes of a Western scale. Music from other cultures often uses scales made up of different tones at different intervals.

Avoid using speech or voice sounds. Instead, use music and composed neutral sounds that would need no translation. Test the sounds with people from your target countries, to see if they carry any adverse cultural connotations.

Scripting considerations

For international distribution, there are two kinds of stacks: those that don't require script localization, and those—usually those with more complex scripts—that do, and cannot run without it.

By following these conventions, you'll make it easier for you or other HyperTalk scripters to localize your stacks for other countries:

- Document your script, algorithms, and any hidden objects.
- Don't make any assumptions about time and date formats.
- Don't embed text in your scripts, such as XFCNs.
- Use English in your scripts.

Document your stacks

Document your scripts, algorithms, and any hidden objects. The more the translators know about your script, the more easily they can make any needed changes. If you will be your own translator, the comments will serve as reminders, long after the project has given way to new ones.

Provide three kinds of documentation: (1) commented scripts; (2) specific high-level descriptions of algorithms, objects, and handlers; and (3) an overall high-level description, listing the stack's objects and control structure. Describe any XCMDs you use and what they do. Many XCMDs are affected by changes in date and time format, printing assumptions, and HyperCard versions.

Don't rely on going back, after you're finished, to insert comments in your script. Write comments as you create the scripts, and then update them when you make modifications.

Time and date formats

Don't make assumptions about time and date formats. Different countries display time and date differently, so both the scripters and users from those countries may incorrectly interpret your time and date information, or not be able to use it at all.

The Macintosh operating system supports many different date and time formats, and HyperCard makes use of this feature. But it's up to you to make sure your stack will work, regardless of the system's date format. For example, the date format for the short date of June 1st, 1988 in HyperTalk is "88.06.01" in Japanese, "01.06.88" in English, and "06.01.88" in Norwegian. The long date is equally varied.

The best way to ensure cross-language compatibility is to use the HyperTalk `dateItems` function. `DateItems` gives you a set of number items indicating the year (in the Roman calendar), month, day, hour, minute, second, and day of the week. To find the name of a month, day, and so on, you can then do a look-up in a table such as a text field. This table should be clearly marked, so the translators don't miss it.

Another approach is to clearly indicate where in your scripts you are making assumptions about date and time formats, and what you are assuming them to be. Or, you could use an XCMD to find out the language of the system you're running on, and then assign formats. Date and time are not the only formats that differ from country to country, but they are among the most frequently used.

Text in scripts

Use the English arguments, especially for the HyperTalk `doMenu` command. The command `doMenu` *menuItemName* for instance, should always use the English *menuItemName,* since all versions of HyperCard in all countries will understand the English.

Don't embed text in your scripts. Instead, store the strings in an invisible text field and then index the field to get the text. This is an inelegant but expedient solution that will make it easier for the translators to find and translate all necessary text. A better solution, eventually, would be to store the strings in resources, and extend HyperTalk itself to be able to access the strings.

Disability Markets

The most salient feature of disability markets is that they differ from each other and in some cases have directly conflicting needs. Decide which specific audiences you are targeting and design to meet their needs.

HyperCard's flexibility and ability to communicate with the serial port and external devices through XCMDs makes it a customizable and useful tool for these markets.

Hearing-impaired

Ten percent of the world's population is hearing-impaired, and computers are extremely accessible to this audience because most computer information is communicated visually. Computers are not only accessible, but they remove any handicap, since everyone using a computer is equally dependent on the visual information.

For hearing-impaired audiences, the most important principle for designing stacks is this: *provide all essential information visually.*

Don't provide voice instructions or information that is only communicated by sound. If you give user feedback with sound, give it visually as well. If you have a specific beep to indicate that an action couldn't be completed, have an accompanying flash as well.

If you are designing a stack for this audience, you can test your stack by turning the sound off in your Control Panel, then using the stack to discover places information is missing.

Visually impaired

Currently, the Macintosh is not highly accessible to the visually impaired population because it does not have an interface that lets the user interact by typing alone, from the moment the machine starts up.

To make your stacks accessible to visually impaired audiences, the most important information is this: *provide all essential information audibly.*

There are two ways to provide audible information. One way is to use sound resources that run on the card's opening or stack's opening, and tell the user what's happening and what to do next. The second way is to use ASCII characters for all screen text. There are "vocoder" devices available that attach to the computer screen, scan for any ASCII screen text, and then vocalize that text. This means using no Paint text, or, if you do use Paint text, putting invisible fields filled with identical ASCII text over the Paint text.

Mobility-impaired

To design for mobility-impaired audiences, you'll need to investigate the particular impairment for which you're designing. Custom HyperCard stacks with touch screens (available from commercial developers) provide a good interface for some audiences, such as people who communicate by tapping keys or screens with a pen-like object held onto their foreheads.

For other audiences, such as those with limited motor control, single serial-key combinations that substitute for double-key combinations are necessary. For people who can't type two keys simultaneously, for instance, it's ordinarily impossible to type an "at" symbol (@), which requires both the Shift key and the 2 key to be pressed at once. Scripting can solve this problem by letting the user type the keys one at a time, and then interpreting the sequence to mean @.

Other audiences might have specialized input devices, such as touch-pads, that could be connected to the Macintosh through the serial port. For these, stacks with XCMDs could provide a good interface.

Summary

The more you are like your target users, the better you will be at predicting their needs. If you are French, for instance, designing a stack for French markets is simple, because you already know what the different colors, sounds, and words connote. Similarly, if you are deaf, you already know a lot about designing a stack for other deaf people.

 If, however, you are designing for an audience of which you are not part, research and user testing are critical. If you are designing for an audience with a specific disability, research that disability and its communication needs thoroughly before designing the stack. During development, test the stack with people who have precisely the disability for which you're designing, to see that your stack meets their needs.

Stack Design Checklist

THIS SECTION CONTAINS TEN SECTIONS OF THE STACK DESIGN CHECKLIST. This worksheet is essentially a collection of checklists and reminders, so that as you build your stack, you have a single reference point. Use the chart in Figure 8-1 to build stacks, the Stack Design Guidelines in Chapter 1 to design their interface, and this worksheet as a quick reference that generally follows and amplifies the guidelines.

Stack Design Checklist

1. Who's your user?

☐ Audience
  Share many characteristics (describe)
  Widely varied
  Describe a typical user (describe two, if your audience has extremes)

☐ Previous experience
  Computers
  Macintosh
  HyperCard
  HyperTalk
  Subject matter expertise

☐ Context in which user will be using the stack
  Alone
  With other software
  With other hardware
  With other stacks
  Over a network
  As part of a training class

☐ Projected machine environment
  Versions of HyperCard
  User level
  Computer models and memory
  Printers
  Ability to work with other stacks

☐ Special markets
  International considerations (and for which countries)
  Disability audiences (and for which disabilities)
  (See Appendix A for more information)

2. What's your subject matter?

☐ What's the general purpose of your stack? (one-sentence summary)

☐ What will your stack cover?

☐ What won't it cover?

☐ How much space do you have to work with?
    Less than 800K
    1 800K disk
    2 800K disks
    1 1.4 megabyte disk
    20 megabytes
    1 CD-ROM disk (656 megabytes)
    Other

☐ What resources do you have to build it with?
    Time
    Developers, graphic designers, sound composers, other
    Money
    Machines and equipment

☐ What is the specific purpose of your stack, given the subject matter's scope, size, space limitations, and your development resources of time, people, and money? Be detailed and explicit.

3. How is it most appropriate to present the subject matter to these users?

☐ What natural sections does your stack divide into?

☐ What functions must it perform?

☐ What's the stack's tone?

☐ What presentation method seems best for these users and this subject matter?
>Slide show
>Demo, with rolling continuous animation
>Training piece, structured and guided
>Desktop presentation, to use while giving a talk
>Game
>Tool, application, or utility
>Other

☐ To the user, will the stack be identifiable as HyperCard? Will the stack's look and feel resemble the Macintosh interface? Will it simulate another kind of software for training purposes? Will it have a completely unique look?

☐ Is there an overall real-world metaphor to support the stack?
>List the things your stack can do
>Look at that list. Is there some real-world object that can also do those things? (Examples: Slide projector, movie, television with channels, supermarket, bank)

4. Is your stack easy to navigate?

☐ Does your stack have navigation buttons on every screen, in same screen location?

☐ Are buttons common to every card separated from card-specific buttons?

☐ Have you provided the user with information about stack structure?
   Context (stack maps, menus, diagrams)
   Location ("You are here" indicators, card names, stack name)
   Options and destinations
   Overall stack structure and layout (metaphor, map, or explicit text)
   A way to tell how much of the stack they've seen (map, menu, progress indicators such as dials or page numbers)

☐ Is there a metaphor that would help the user comprehend your stack's navigation more easily?
   A metaphor with parts, such as a notebook with tabbed sections
   A metaphor that implies your stack's structure and navigation, such as a slide projector, cassette recorder, customized control panel

☐ Have you chosen an appropriate stack structure?
   Single-frame
      Display
      Filter
      See-and-point
   Linear
      Jump-linear
   Tree
   Network
   Combination

5. Does your stack have a proper introduction?

☐ Does your stack include the following introductory elements?
    Initial screen stating name and purpose
    Introduction or opening
    Stack-specific help
    Something for the user to do right away
    A home base or reference point, such as a menu or stack map

☐ Can the users learn about the stack?
    Purpose
    Content
    Structure and extent
    Options
    Assumptions

☐ When you test the stack, do people use it correctly?
    Use the help function (instead of ignoring it)
    Use the stack correctly (instead of overlooking options or functions)
    Comment positively (instead of muttering in frustration)
    Use the stack right away (instead of spending visible learning time)
    Go through the stack smoothly (instead of all making the same error)

6. Graphics

☐ What is your visual look? (Some examples are businesslike, medieval, art-deco, childlike, Macintosh or other software simulation, future tech)

☐ Is your design best suited to one stack or several? One background or several?

☐ How have you planned your card layout?
> Underlying grid pattern
> Allowance made for text, illustrations, background graphics, and visible buttons
> Edges of the grid used for permanent buttons

☐ Have you put elements common to most or all cards in the background?

☐ Which of the following will you need to design?
> Buttons and icons
> Fields
> Backgrounds
> Illustrations
> Scanned images
> Animation sequences
> Screen titles

☐ How have you planned your typography?
> Font styles that visually match the tone of your stack
> Fonts big enough and dark enough to be easily readable
> Text laid out in a grid
> Line width and line spacing that make text readable

7. Writing

☐ How polished and appropriate is your writing?
Concise expression
Works with graphics to convey meaning
Works with sound to convey meaning
Flows well from screen to screen; sounds good if read aloud
Is sufficiently independent on each screen so that users can tell
what's meant
Has the right tone for your audience (not condescending or punitive)
Has been checked for accuracy and editorial correctness

8. Sound

☐ Do you tell the user how to deal with sound?
Instructions for turning sound down in Control Panel
Instructions (and button) for turning sound off completely
Instructions to install stack on user's hard disk (if this is necessary for
your stack's sounds)

☐ Are sounds associated with the stack's operation in a consistent way?
Visual effects
Major navigation transitions
The stack's content
User feedback
Progress indicators
A running sound track

☐ Have you tested sounds completely?
On all intended machines with all possible configurations of RAM and
disk space
With and without a hard disk
At different volume levels
With several repetitions, to make sure sounds are not annoying

9. Testing

☐ Test several times during the design and development of your stack

☐ Don't tell testers how to do the thing you're testing for

☐ Guidelines for testing

    Set an objective

    Design the specific tasks that use the things you want to test

        Navigation

        Use of stack

        Buttons

        Entire stack: How do they use it

    Decide how to record user trials

    Determine the setting (microphones, recorders, videotape, no distractions)

    Find representative users that are like your target audience

☐ Ten steps for conducting a test:

1. Introduce yourself.

2. Describe the purpose of the test, in general terms.

3. Tell participants it's all right to quit at any time.

4. Talk about the equipment in the room.

5. Explain how to "think aloud." Tell them if they forget, you'll remind them.

6. Explain that you will not provide help.

7. Describe the tasks and introduce the stack. Tell them how to start it up, unless start-up is something you're testing.

8. Ask if the user has any questions before you start. Then begin.

9. Run the test and finish it.

10. Use the results.

☐ Test to see that the following situations don't occur:
    User gets to a screen without buttons or textual navigation reminders
    User can't tell which objects are buttons
    User can't tell what buttons do
    User gets lost
    User misses large portions of the stack
    User is confused early or often
    User breaks stack
    User develops clumsy way to use stack instead of the intended way
    Several users make mistakes at same spot or miss the same point
    You give user verbal hints, and so never discover how a lone user would fare
    A stack to which yours connects can't be found

☐ Test the stack yourself by intentionally doing things that a first-time user might do wrong:
    Type at random on the keyboard
    Do the opposite of the stack's purpose
    Go random places from various cards
    Click and type ahead
    Click several times in the same spot on one button

10. Checking your stack

☐ Check your stack on all intended machines with all possible memory configurations
    Macintosh Plus
    Macintosh SE
    Macintosh II, with various amounts of memory
    Each model with a hard disk, if your stack must be installed

☐ Check animation
    Speed and appearance on slowest and fastest intended machines
    Smoothness
    Visual impact
    Coordination with sound

☐ Check visual effects for consistency

☐ Check sound
    Volume
    Pace
    Smoothness
    Pleasantness even with repetition
    Adherence to the stack's tone and mood

☐ Check writing
    Flow
    Typographical and grammatical correctness
    Consistent font usage
    Accuracy

□ Check that buttons are where they should be and do what they're supposed to do on every card

□ Check that cards are in logical sequential order

□ Check that scripts and XCMDs work

□ Compact the stack

Recommended Reading

THIS SECTION CONTAINS A VARIETY OF GRAPHIC AND INTERFACE DESIGN books, from several fields, that you may find useful in designing your stacks.

The books are divided into the following categories:

- charts and diagrams
- creative process
- drawing and visual thinking
- film, television, and animation
- graphic design and layout
- graphic styles
- human–computer user interface
- HyperCard books by Apple authors
- symbols and icons
- typography
- visual references and image libraries
- writing

Charts and diagrams

Robertson, Bruce. *How to Draw Charts and Diagrams*. Cincinnati: North Light Books, 1988. Provides a reference for the main kinds of charts. The book covers in detail charts of relationships; charts of quantities; graphs; and maps.

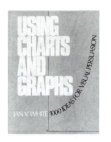

White, Jan V. *Using Charts and Graphs: 1000 Ideas for Visual Persuasion*. New York: R. R. Bowker, 1984. Explains and illustrates the nuances of charting. This book discusses pie charts, bar charts, dot charts, line charts, flow charts, maps, tables, and frames.

Creative process

Hanks, Kurt, and Jay A. Parry. *Wake Up Your Creative Genius*. Los Altos, CA: William Kaufman, 1983. Presents techniques for and examples of creative thinking. The book consists of several two-page chapters discussing how to stimulate, expand, nurture, and protect new ideas.

von Oech, Roger. *A Whack on the Side of the Head: How to Unlock Your Mind for Innovation*. Menlo Park, CA: Creative Think, 1982. Focuses on creating new ideas. The book is divided into ten chapters, each of which gives techniques for temporarily setting aside a specific belief, such as "Be practical" or "To err is wrong," in the interests of stimulating creativity.

Drawing and visual thinking

Guptill, Arthur L. *Rendering in Pencil*. New York: Watson-Guptill, 1977. Presents basic techniques for rendering objects realistically in pencil. The book discusses using line, tone, outline, light, and perspective, particularly in rendering objects of nature or of architecture.

Hanks, Kurt, and Jerry Belliston. *Draw! A Visual Approach to Thinking, Learning and Communicating*. Los Altos, CA: William Kaufman, 1977. Assumes that anyone can already draw and introduces techniques such as "overlapping" and "perspective" to improve existing skill. The book also covers drawing as a way to visualize, create, learn, and communicate.

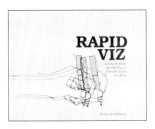

Hanks, Kurt, and Jerry Belliston. *Rapid Viz: A New Method for the Rapid Visualization of Ideas*. Los Altos, CA: William Kaufman, 1980. Presents drawing as a way of capturing ideas quickly and casually, not as a means of producing finished illustration. The book shows how simple techniques such as "contour drawing" can make drawing a more useful tool for anyone.

McKim, Robert H. *Experiences in Visual Thinking, Second Edition*. Boston: P.W.S. Publishers Co., 1980. Discusses thinking and introduces drawing as a means of strengthening the thinking process. The book weaves together research findings, citations for further reading, quotations, mental exercises, and drawing techniques.

Film, television, and animation

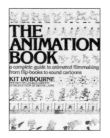

Laybourne, Kit. *The Animation Book: A Complete Guide to Animated Filmmaking—From Flip-books to Sound Cartoons.* New York: Crown, 1979. Discusses all aspects of modern animation: basic skills, animation techniques, tools needed, and resources available. The chapters on basic skills and storyboarding are the especially useful for stack design.

Merritt, Douglas. *Television Graphics: From Pencil to Pixel.* New York: Van Nostrand Reinhold, 1987. Focuses on the role of graphics and computer graphics in television. This is a heavily illustrated book, discussing topics such as title sequences, station identity, storyboards, stills, visual effects, and computer-aided animation.

Muybridge, Eadweard. *Animals in Motion.* New York: Dover, 1957. Shows step-by-step photographs of 34 different animals in 123 kinds of motion. This is a selection of plates from the 1887 original work. These illustrations are useful to anyone creating animations of animals.

Muybridge, Eadweard. *The Human Figure in Motion.* New York: Dover, 1955. Shows step-by-step photographs of 163 different kinds of human actions. Like *Animals in Motion,* this is a selection of plates from the 1887 original work. These illustrations are useful to anyone creating animations of people.

Thomas, Frank, and Ollie Johnston. *Disney Animation: The Illusion of Life.* New York: Abbeville, 1981. Presents the animation techniques as they evolved at the Disney studios. This 575-page book, heavily illustrated with Disney characters, covers animation's evolution since 1923 and discusses aspects such as story, character development, backgrounds, and animation techniques.

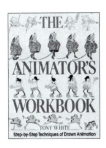

White, Tony. *The Animator's Workbook: Step-by-Step Techniques of Drawn Animation.* New York: Watson-Guptill, 1986. Focuses on the drawing techniques needed to portray animated cartoon motion. This book focuses on the details of animating walks, runs, head turns, and exaggerated actions.

Zettl, Herbert. *Sight • Sound • Motion: Applied Media Aesthetics.* Belmont, CA: Wadsworth, 1973. Discusses how to effectively incorporate sight, sound, and motion. The book explores using light, two-dimensional and three-dimensional space, time-motion, and sound. It includes illustrations from television and film.

Graphic design and layout

Berryman, Gregg. *Notes on Graphic Design and Visual Communication.* Los Altos, CA: William Kaufmann, 1984. Provides a brief summary of the basics of graphic design. Only 46 pages, this book provides simple rules of thumb for graphic design, symbols, layout, and grids.

Book, Albert C., and C. Dennis Schick. *Fundamentals of Copy and Layout: Everything You Need to Know to Prepare Better Ads*. Lincolnwood, IL: NTC Business Books, 1986. Discusses the layout of text and graphics in print, radio, storyboard, and television formats. This book addresses some concerns of stack designers such as editing text, integrating text and graphics, and designing layout.

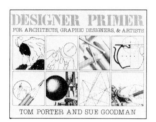

Gill, Bob. *Forget All the Rules You Ever Learned About Graphic Design. Including the Ones in This Book*. New York: Watson-Guptill, 1981. Presents eight rules for design, each followed by several examples. The rules include "Interesting words need boring graphics," "Boring words need interesting graphics," "Stealing is good," "Less is more," and "More is more."

Porter, Tom, and Sue Goodman. *Designer Primer: for Architects, Graphic Designers, and Artists*. New York: Charles Scribner's Sons, 1988. Provides techniques for drawing and drafting by hand. This book consists of one-page explanations covering all aspects of visual perception, media, freehand drawing techniques, design graphics, and image-building issues. Reprinted by permission of Charles Scribner's Sons, an imprint of Macmillan Publishing Company from the cover of *Designer Primer* by Tom Porter and Sue Goodman. Copyright © 1988 Macmillan Publishing Company, a division of Macmillan, Inc.

White, Jan V. *Editing by Design: A Guide to Effective Word-and-Picture Communication for Editors and Designers*. New York: R. R. Bowker, 1982. Focuses on how to use text and graphics together in a layout or grid. The book also discusses type, illustrations, and color as additional elements.

White, Jan V. *Graphic Idea Notebook: Inventive Techniques for Designing Printed Pages*. New York: Watson-Guptill, 1980. Shows hundreds of graphic ideas and is intended to be a quick reference for the designer in need of immediate solutions. Gives techniques for getting attention, changing direction, using boxes, and breaking up text.

Wilde, Richard. *Problems: Solutions: Visual Thinking for Graphic Communicators*. New York: Van Nostrand Reinhold, 1986. Shows 53 problems and over 550 original graphic solutions. The book presents each problem, gives the reader a chance to consider the problem, then shows not one but several good solutions.

Graphic styles

Hamm, Jack. *Cartooning the Head and Figure*. New York: Putnam, 1967. Illustrates cartooning techniques and gives hundreds of examples. This slim paperback shows how to cartoon faces, hands, feet, clothing, standing and walking figures, athletes in action, babies, and old people.

Heller, Steven, and Seymour Chwast. *Graphic Styles: From Victorian to Post-Modern*. New York: Harry N. Abrams, 1988. Shows graphic styles since the Industrial Revolution. The book discusses the main graphic styles: Victorian, arts and crafts, art nouveau, early modern, expressionist, art deco, dada, heroic realism, late modern, and post-modern.

Meggs, Philip B. *A History of Graphic Design*. New York: Van Nostrand Reinhold, 1983. Presents graphic styles from prehistoric times through the present. The book is a compendium of illustrations, anecdotes, and lively history. It provides a rich reference of graphic styles for the searching stack designer.

Human–computer user interface

Apple Computer, Inc. *Human Interface Guidelines: The Apple Desktop Interface*. Reading, MA: Addison-Wesley, 1987. Describes the philosophy and elements of Apple's desktop interface. Most of the book describes in detail each element of the desktop interface, including windows and menus, and the specifications of how each element must act.

Shneiderman, Ben. *Designing the User Interface: Strategies for Effective Human-Computer Interaction*. Reading, MA: Addison-Wesley, 1987. Integrates research from computer science and psychology and presents principles for interface design; includes extensive bibliography. The book discusses human factors of interactive software, selection systems, response rate, on-line help, and iterative design and testing.

HyperCard books by Apple authors

Ambron, SueAnn, and Kristina Hooper, eds. *Interactive Multimedia: Visions of Multimedia for Developers, Educators, and Information Providers*. Redmond, WA: Microsoft Press, 1988. Presents a collection of essays on interactive multimedia. The essays discuss multimedia in computer science, education, television, and publishing, and speculate about its future use. The epilogue focuses on HyperCard.

Apple Computer, Inc. *HyperCard Script Language Guide: The HyperTalk Language.* Reading, MA: Addison-Wesley, 1988. Provides a technical reference to the HyperTalk scripting language. The book defines objects, messages, values, keywords, system messages, commands, functions, properties, and constants used in the language.

Kaehler, Carol. *HyperCard Power: Techniques and Scripts.* Reading, MA: Addison-Wesley, 1988. Discusses building stacks. This book, written by the author of HyperCard's original Help system, was one of the first published on HyperCard. It describes how to customize and author stacks and is full of hints for the beginner.

Symbols and icons

Dreyfuss, Henry. *Symbol Sourcebook: An Authoritative Guide to International Graphic Symbols.* New York: Van Nostrand Reinhold, 1984. Shows thousands of symbols, presented first by subject, then by shape, and finally in the index by name. This book is a fertile source for the stack designer seeking icons or other stylized design images.

Holmes, Nigel, with Rose DeNeve. *Designing Pictorial Symbols.* New York: Watson-Guptill, 1985. Presents 54 case studies of how concepts were transformed into icons. This book is useful because it not only shows the finished icon, but it explains the stages and thoughts that the designer went through to create each icon.

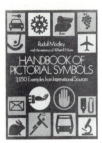

Modley, Rudolf, with William R. Myers. *Handbook of Pictorial Symbols: 3250 Examples from International Sources*. New York: Dover, 1976. Illustrates over 3000 symbols. Like many other books published by Dover, this one encourages you to use its graphics. On the copyright page, it gives permission to use any ten symbols in one piece, providing you follow the other restrictions on the page, and it encourages you to write for permission to use more.

Typography

Carter, Rob, Ben Day, and Philip Meggs. *Typographic Design: Form and Communication*. New York: Van Nostrand Reinhold, 1985. Describes the evolution and function of typography and illustrates several typefaces in different sizes. Devoted almost entirely to print technology, this book provides a thorough understanding of typography's roots.

Romano, Frank J. *The TypEncyclopedia: A User's Guide to Better Typography*. New York: R.R. Bowker, 1976. Defines and illustrates typographic terms. This book makes a useful reference tool, with each page cleanly illustrating one term. It covers topics such as calligraphy, ellipses, italics, ligatures, ornaments, and serif typefaces.

Visual references and image libraries

Bragonier, Reginald, Jr., and David Fisher. *What's What: A Visual Glossary of Everyday Objects—From Paper Clips to Passenger Ships*. Maplewood, NJ: Hammond, Inc., 1981. Shows pictures of objects, naming all the parts of each object. The book is organized by physical categories such as the earth, living things, shelters, the arts, machinery, and symbols. The book's scope and thorough index make it a valuable source of both images and words.

The Diagram Group. *Comparisons*. New York: St. Martin's, 1980. Compares similar objects using both text and illustrations. The topics include distance, size, temperature, and speed. One spread compares animal speeds in air, in water, and on land, for instance. This book is useful not only as a reference, but also as a model of graphic solutions.

Grafton, Carol Belanger, ed. *1001 Floral Motifs and Ornaments for Artists and Craftspeople*. NewYork: Dover, 1987. Contains floral illustrations suitable for scanning. Like many Dover books, this one encourages you to use its graphics. It gives permission to use any ten illustrations in one piece, providing you follow the other restrictions described, and encourages you to write for permission to use more.

Grafton, Carol Belanger, ed. *Pictorial Archive of Printer's Ornaments from the Renaissance to the 20th Century*. NewYork: Dover, 1980. Presents 1489 designs, borders, and headings. Like many Dover books, this one encourages you to use its graphics.

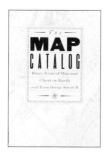

Makower, Joel, ed., with Laura Bergheim. *The Map Catalog: Every Kind of Map and Chart on Earth and Even Some Above It*. New York: Vintage, 1986. Shows maps of the land, sky, and water depicting many kinds of information. This book is not only a geographical reference book, but is also a source book for ideas about stack maps and other perceptual maps.

Tierney, Tom, ed. *Illustrations of Hands*. New York: Dover, 1983. Illustrates over 370 hands. Like many Dover books, this one encourages you to use its graphics. The designs here are copyright-free and you are encouraged to use ten or fewer in any one piece, or write for permission to use more.

Writing

Elbow, Peter. *Writing with Power: Techniques for Mastering the Writing Process*. New York: Oxford University, 1981. Introduces ways to write and revise that will strengthen, not strangle, your voice. The book discusses techniques for separating writing from revising, for addressing an audience, for using feedback, and for writing with power.

Strunk, Jr., William, and E. B. White. *The Elements of Style, Third Edition*. New York: Macmillan, 1979. Gives a few memorable rules for writing well. The book is short and covers the survival elements of usage, composition, and style. The guidelines, such as "Omit needless words" and "Revise and rewrite," are clear. Reprinted with permission of Macmillan Publishing Company from *The Elements of Style* by William Strunk, Jr. and E.B. White. Copyright © 1979 by Macmillan Publishing Company.

Shulevitz, Uri. *Writing with Pictures: How to Write and Illustrate Children's Books*. New York: Watson-Guptill, 1985. Describes how to create children's stories. The most useful part of this book for stack designers is the chapter on "Telling a Story," which discusses which elements any story must have, how to space that story over several pages or screens, and how to balance words with pictures.

University of Chicago Press, the Editorial Staff. *The Chicago Manual of Style, Thirteenth Edition*. Chicago: University of Chicago, 1982. Provides a complete reference for English punctuation, usage, and style. The most pertinent part of the book for stack designers is Part 2, "Style," which supplies guidelines appropriate for any written text.

Glossary

About box: The text that appears when the About icon button is clicked, giving information about a stack's creators. The About icon looks like a cartoon speech balloon and is available in the Button Info dialog box.

"attract-mode" opening: An inviting, animated, possibly audible stack opening whose purpose is to attract people to the machine. The opening plays repeatedly until someone clicks the mouse. Compare **static opening.**

CD-ROM disc: A compact disc that can store 656 megabytes of audio, video, or digital computer information, but whose information—like music on a record album—cannot be changed. The initials stand for *compact disc read-only memory.*

combination structure: A **stack structure** that combines two or more standard structures. For example, a stack might use a **single-frame structure** to let the user choose a topic, then a **tree structure** to let the user learn about that topic.

configuration: See **machine configuration.**

custom icon: An icon that is not one of the standard icons available in the Button Info dialog box. Custom icons are created using a program such as MacPaint and a resource editor such as ResEdit or IconMaker. See also **icon, icon button.**

display stack: A kind of **single-frame** stack that devotes most of its card space to a single display area. The user clicks to select what will be shown in that display.

external command: See **XCMD.**

field text: See **regular text.**

filter stack: A kind of **single-frame** stack that lets the user sort through information using "filters" to specify the kind of information sought. A stack of Canadian animals, for example, might let the user filter by kind of animal and thus sort for only the mammals in the stack.

final disk: The fully-tested final version of a stack, from which all other copies will be duplicated.

font: A complete set of characters in one design, size, and style.

front end: Software which is put "in front" of other software to make the latter accessible or easier to use. A stack that consists mostly of data, for instance, may contain a front end with which to search the data. Or, an entire stack may function as a front end to another software application.

grid: An invisible layout that divides a card into separate visual areas.

help system: A card or cards, created by the stack designer, that give stack-specific information. Stack-specific help is different from HyperCard's generic Help system, and is often given another name, such as "How to use this stack," to clarify the difference.

icon: A stylized image that graphically conveys purpose or function. For example, the right-arrow icon is used on buttons that take the user forward in the stack, and the house icon is used on buttons which take the user to the Home card.

icon button: A button that uses a graphic icon to convey the button's meaning. The icon may be one of the standard icons available through the Button Info dialog box, or may be a **custom icon.**

interface: The elements that make up a stack's presentation, rather than its function. *Visual interface* refers to the graphic elements; *audio interface* refers to the stack's sound elements; *user interface* refers to all the elements taken together.

iterative development: The process of building a version of a stack, getting reviews, revising the stack, and then repeating the cycle as many times as needed.

jump-linear structure: A variation of the **linear structure** that provides both a linear sequence and a single "home-base" from which the user can jump to any new destination and return. (Technically, this structure is a form of **tree structure,** but it gets its name from the fact that users perceive it as primarily linear.)

linear structure: A form of **stack structure** which encourages and possibly forces the user to move through it in a straight line. A slide-show stack might use a linear structure.

machine configuration: The exact combination of Macintosh model, RAM, disk space, and monitor that a user possesses.

map: See **stack map.**

menu: A list of stack sections. It may be graphic, textual, or both, and is frequently the stack's central reference point. Not to be confused with the command menus available in the menu bar.

metaphor: An identification between a real-world object and parts of your stack that share the object's characteristics. The standard Macintosh interface, for example, uses a desktop metaphor with documents, file folders, and trash cans.

MIDI: Acronym for *Musical Instrument Digital Interface,* a communications format used by computers and some electronic instruments to exchange information.

navigation: The elements of the stack's interface that allow a user to orient and travel within the stack. Navigation provides information about what's available, where the user is in the stack, where the user can go, where the user has already been, and how to travel. See also **user interface.**

network structure: A form of **stack structure** that presents information in sections that are not hierarchically related. A stack representing airline routes, for example, might use a network structure.

Paint text: Text you type using the Paint Text tool. The tool is represented on the Paint menu by a capital letter A. Paint text can appear anywhere, while **regular text** must appear in a field created with the Field tool.

progress indicator: A graphic symbol, such as a dial or gauge, that is always present and shows the user how much of the stack has been seen.

prototype: A preliminary version of the stack that indicates what the final intended version will contain. Graphics, text, animation, and scripts are described, though perhaps not present. A prototype's purpose is to stimulate useful review comments for the stack designer.

regular text: Text you type inside a field. You use the Browse tool to set an insertion point in a field and then type. Regular text is editable and searchable, while **Paint text** is not.

review: A set of comments by selected people on the stack's design, appearance, and function. A review is usually less formal and less structured than **user testing.**

sampler: A piece of software, possibly with some additional hardware, that enables the computer to record sound wholly, like a tape recorder.

scanner: A device that copies images into the computer. A flatbed scanner works like a copy machine, and will scan any object placed on its surface. A video digitizer will scan any object within a video camera's view.

see-and-point stack: A form of **single-frame structure** that presents general information on one card. The user clicks on different areas of the card to learn more. A map of stars that enlarges any clicked constellation, for example, is a see-and-point stack.

sequencer: A piece of software, possibly with additional hardware, that enables the computer to manipulate and program stored sounds to create melodies.

single-frame structure: A form of **stack structure** in which all action appears to take place within a single card and navigation appears to be nonexistent. See also **display stack, filter stack, and see-and-point stack.**

stack map: A representation, usually graphic, of the stack's parts, the relationship of those parts, and the stack structure. Most stack maps are "live," so that the user can go to any part of the stack by clicking on the appropriate part of the map.

stack structure: The perceived order and relationship of a stack's cards. The structure may be **linear, network, single-frame, tree,** or a **combination** of these.

static opening: A stack opening that displays a title screen, possibly followed by credit information and then by the main menu. It may include a short, animated opening before the title screen and menu appear. Compare **"attract-mode" opening.**

textual reminder: Written directions informing the user of available options, particularly **navigation** options.

target machine: The **machine configuration** upon which your stack is intended to run. Some stacks are designed to run on every Macintosh model in every configuration, and thus have several target machines. Others, such as demo stacks, may be designed only for high-end Macintosh computers with color monitors and the maximum amount of RAM.

test: To check a stack to make sure it works and is complete. The term "test" is sometimes used informally to refer to **user testing,** as well.

travel button: A button whose purpose is to let the user move around within the stack.

tree structure: A form of **stack structure** that presents information in sections that are hierarchically related. A stack showing a family's genealogy might use a tree structure.

typography: The visual appearance of text. Typography includes elements such as font, alignment, line width, and line height.

user interface: All the elements that make up how a stack looks and how a user interacts with it. The user interface elements include the graphics, text, and sound that make up the presentation and navigation; they do not include the stack's functionality.

user level: The setting on the User Preferences card in the Home stack that lets you use HyperCard's tools and capabilities. Five user levels are available: Browsing, Typing, Painting, Authoring, and Scripting.

user testing: The process of selecting people who either are like your stack's intended users or who possess relevant expertise, defining what you want to learn from them, and observing them use your stack. "User testing" is sometimes used less formally to mean "getting reviews from people who are like your stack's intended users."

XCMD: Abbreviation for *external command;* program written in another language, such as C or Pascal, that can be called from within HyperCard. Custom XCMDs can extend HyperCard's capabilities to include any function a Macintosh can perform.

Index